THE
UNKNOWN
COURIER

THE UNKNOWN COURIER

THE TRUE STORY OF OPERATION MINCEMEAT

IAN COLVIN

Biteback Publishing

This edition published in Great Britain in 2016 by
Biteback Publishing Ltd
Westminster Tower
3 Albert Embankment
London SE1 7SP

ISBN 978-1-78590-137-9

10 9 8 7 6 5 4 3 2 1

A CIP catalogue record for this book is available from the British Library.

Set in Albertina and Bureau Grotesque by Adrian McLaughlin

Printed and bound in Great Britain by
CPI Group (UK) Ltd, Croydon CR0 4YY

To my friend

Cyril M. Armitage, M.V.O., M.A., R.N.V.R.

sometime Chaplain to the Royal Marines,
Vicar of St. Bride's Church, Fleet Street,
this journalist's enquiry into the strange enlistment
of Major William Martin, Royal Marines,
is dedicated

WAS YOUR JOURNEY REALLY NECESSARY?

Rommel arriving in Salonika on 25 July 1943, in consequence of Hitler's
reaction to the papers found on the body of the courier

CONTENTS

ACKNOWLEDGEMENTS

I am grateful to the Ministry of Defence for the facilities given to me and for permission to reproduce the unusual documents contained in this book. My thanks are also due to the Admiralty for the loan of copies of the *Führer Conferences on Naval Affairs*, and to the Public Relations Officers of the Service Ministries and the Foreign Office for assistance in my enquiries. I must also acknowledge my indebtedness to a number of contemporary authors, some of whose works I have quoted. Their books are mentioned in the list of sources contained in the Bibliography.

In publishing the patrol report of H.M. Submarine *Seraph* my thanks are due to Commander N. L. A. Jewell, M.B.E., D.S.C., R.N.

I should like to pay tribute by name to all the officials responsible for the conception and carrying out of the plan, but for security reasons this is not permissible, though it has been disclosed that the Hon. Ewen Montagu, Q.C., was the executive naval officer in charge of it. The highly reputable solicitors, bankers, clubs, hotels and others whose names were used in the documents for the purpose of deceiving the enemy, were not, of course, in reality associated with the operation. Apart from my fellow journalist,

Julian, there are only three persons in this narrative who are given 'cover' names.

Two of them are the German ex-intelligence officers who were at the receiving end of Operation 'Mincemeat' and who have especially asked me to use their pseudonyms, as they are now carrying on peaceable occupations in Spain. The third man to whom I have given a pseudonym is Don Alvarez Peters, one of their rivals in the British service.

IAN COLVIN

FOREWORD

The Double Cross System was one of the most successful and valuable intelligence operations of the Second World War, probably only second to Bletchley Park's ability to break the German and Japanese codes. Nazi spies operating in Britain or against the allies in mainland Europe were recruited as double agents by MI5 and MI6 and played back against the Germans, feeding them false intelligence that would lead them to make decisions on the battlefield that played into the allies' hands. These operations were coordinated by the Double Cross Committee, which was made up of representatives from MI5, MI6 and the armed forces intelligence departments.

The most important and complex of these 'deception' operations was deployed to fool the Germans into believing that the D-Day landings would be on the Pas de Calais and that the Normandy attacks were simply a feint attack designed to draw German troops away from the main landing sites. As a result, Hitler ordered two armoured divisions that were on their way to reinforce the German troops in Normandy back to Calais, a move that may well have ensured that the Allied troops were not thrown back into the sea.

The successful D-Day deception plan was presaged by a much less complex deception carried out ahead of Operation Husky: the invasion in July 1943 of Sicily. Codenamed 'Mincemeat', the cover plan involved planting a dead body, the 'Unknown Courier' of the title of this book, in the sea off the coast of Spain. The body was to look as if it was from an aircraft which had crashed into the sea. Dressed as a military officer, it would be carrying a briefcase containing correspondence between senior officers involved in the planning which would suggest that Operation Husky was not just the beginning of the invasion of Italy but an invasion of southern Europe with the initial landings taking place not in Sicily but in Sardinia and Greece.

One of the most underestimated elements of the Double Cross System is the role of Bletchley Park. The ability of Bletchley to break the German secret service codes ensured that the British could be certain that the Germans believed the false, and sometimes fantastic, intelligence the double agents were sending to Berlin. Without the confidence that gave the Allied generals that the Germans believed the fake stories, they could not have incorporated them into their plans. Yet, as a result of the extreme secrecy surrounding Bletchley's role, this indispensable element of the Double Cross deceptions, including Mincemeat, only emerged in the 1990s.

Noel Currer-Briggs, an intelligence officer at Bletchley Park, was sent out to produce reports from a mobile army signals intelligence unit based in Tunisia, which was to be the springboard for the invasion of Sicily. In May 1943, they were visited by the Allied commander, US General Dwight Eisenhower, and British General Harold Alexander. 'We were stationed at Bizerta on top of a hill just outside Tunis and I remember we were inspected one day by Alexander and Eisenhower,' Currer-Briggs said.

There we were working away at the German wireless traffic coming from the other side of the Mediterranean and we were saying:

'Oh yes. They've moved that division from Sicily to Sardinia and they've moved the other one to the Balkans' and these two generals were jumping up and down like a couple of schoolboys at a football match. We hadn't a clue why. We thought: 'Silly old buffers'.

Churchill, whose characteristically unconventional involvement in Mincemeat is described in the Appendix, was in Washington for talks with President Franklin D. Roosevelt, when he received the message: 'Mincemeat swallowed whole.'

The elaborate Mincemeat deception, of which this is the earliest true account, makes such a gripping story that Ewen Montagu, the naval intelligence officer on the Double Cross Committee, who, with his air force intelligence colleague Charles Cholmondeley, was responsible for devising it, wanted to publish it immediately the war came to an end. He was refused permission.

In 1950, Duff Cooper, a member of Churchill's wartime cabinet, wrote a novel, *Operation Heartbreak*, which was loosely based on the Mincemeat operation. Ian Colvin, a journalist with the *Daily Telegraph*, heard that Cooper's book was based on fact and set out to investigate. Colvin was well placed to do so. He had worked in Berlin before the war as a correspondent for the *News Chronicle*, but had also passed information to both the MI6 head of station Frank Foley and Churchill, who at the time was in the political wilderness. Britain's wartime Prime Minister later recorded that Colvin 'plunged very deeply into German politics and established contacts of a most secret character with some of the important German generals, and also with independent men of character and quality in Germany who saw in the Hitler Movement the approaching ruin of their land'. Colvin was expelled in 1939 and after the war became a foreign correspondent for the *Daily Telegraph*.

Colvin's account of Mincemeat is an intriguing mix of intelligence and detective work, as information collected from his intelligence contacts and the mysterious 'hush men' leads him to Madrid, Gibraltar, Seville and finally to a modest grave in Huelva, the last resting place of *The Unknown Courier*.

What should have been a major bestseller was stymied at the last moment by the publication of Montagu's own book, *The Man Who Never Was*, which stole Colvin's thunder. It was long believed that Britain's intelligence services were panicked by the news that a journalist had got hold of the story, and decided to get their own version out, giving Montagu permission to publish so long as he carefully omitted any mention of the role of Bletchley Park. But when the official files were released, it became clear that the intelligence authorities were in fact furious with Montagu for breaking his oath of secrecy. The files also revealed that many of the naval intelligence documents on Operation Mincemeat were marked with the codeword HUSH, offering the intriguing possibility that Montagu was one of those mysterious 'hush men' briefing Colvin, and that he had done so in order to 'get the story out there' so that he could publish his own account. Whatever the truth, Colvin's quest for it, which leads him to Nazi spies, Spanish flamenco dancers and even a 'frogman pathologist', makes a fascinating read.

MICHAEL SMITH
Editor of the Dialogue Espionage Classics series
September 2016

A NOTE

ON THE SITUATION CONFRONTING
THE AXIS IN THE MEDITERRANEAN
IN THE SPRING OF 1943

by

FIELD-MARSHAL KESSELRING

Then Commander-in-Chief South

By the annihilation and capture of the Axis forces in North Africa the Allies had won freedom of movement in the Mediterranean. In spite of the uncomfortable narrows between Tunis and the Italian islands, Pantellaria, Sicily and Sardinia, the crossing could be regarded as sufficiently secured in view of the increasingly conspicuous inactivity of the Italian navy. The Axis air forces were a factor of diminishing importance.

The next move of the Allied forces was bound to reveal their ultimate objectives. The continuation of the war against Italy might have as its objective her defeat and elimination, but also the conquest of a new base for offensives against the German eastern and western fronts and the central citadel of Germany itself.

Eventual landings in the south of France or in the Balkans, especially in conjunction with a reinforcement of the Allied strength in the Mediterranean, might be assessed as a preliminary to operations with far-reaching strategic and political aims.

Since January 1943 I had been giving serious thought to these problems. I had formed a clear picture from information personally collected and from conferences with the Italian commanders on the islands, and had obtained from the German and Italian High Commands their approval for the first essential measures to meet the situation. There was good reason for urgency. The optimism displayed by the island commanders was not proof against a sober examination of the facts. On the maps everything was in order, their plans cleverly thought out, in some respects too cleverly by half. But the only construction work done was mere eyewash. There were no prepared positions on the islands, which were inadequately defended, and had unguarded tank obstacles more likely to hamper the defenders than to check the enemy – all so much gingerbread.

The coastal divisions I inspected were on a par with the fortifications. With such troops in these defences it was hopeless to offer resistance. There were differences: Corsica was the best, then came Sardinia; Sicily and the Calabrian coast left much to be desired. In April I turned the heat on which, in view of Lt.-Gen. Ambrosio's hostile attitude, was only possible by tactful co-operation with subordinate departments. I made sure that the commanders of the islands were willingly carrying out my suggestions within the limits of their material and ability. The supplies that were gradually made available by the O.K.W. were inadequate despite their quantity. Their distribution was determined by the expected strategic intentions of the enemy. I summed up the situation briefly as follows:

The occupation of the north coast of Africa could not be regarded as a final objective even if the annihilation of two armies justified the Allied expenditure of force in North Africa. The military defeat of the Axis forces there was a necessary preliminary to any further move and to the realisation of the 'Casablanca Plans' about which at that time we had no detailed information.

The conglomeration of British and American forces in the Tunisian area indicated first and foremost that the Allies intended to prosecute their operations in the west Mediterranean. Sicily lay within striking distance; the capture of the island would be an important step on the road to Italy. At the same time a diversionary assault on Calabria as complementary to the occupation of Sicily had to be reckoned with. As Pantellaria was incapable of putting up any show of resistance, its occupation had only a secondary importance. The enemy would gain more from an operation against Sardinia and Corsica if the Allied objective were the speedy capture of Rome. The effect on the Axis forces in Sicily and southern Italy of a successful assault on those islands was not to be underrated. On the other hand the Allies could not leave out of account the threat to their flank from Sicily, the extent of which it would be difficult to gauge. The possession of the islands, especially Corsica as an 'aircraft-carrier', would facilitate an offensive directed against the south of France.

For an operation in the eastern Mediterranean the Allied forces in Tunis were far away. But the difficulties could be overcome. The Balkans could be reached across the Italian mainland; motorised units could be sent forward by road to Tripoli, Benghazi or Tobruk, and from there transported to the Aegean. The Allies knew that they need anticipate very little resistance on the sea. On the other hand, the combat air forces on the island of Crete, in the Peloponnese, round Athens and Salonika, weak though they then were, could easily be reinforced and presented a potentially effective defence in depth to which the Allies could only with difficulty oppose an equal strength. But if the Allies were to land in the Balkans and launch an offensive against the rear of the German eastern front with the objective of joining up with the Russians their success would not only affect the military situation; it would have political repercussions of at least equal importance.

Thus there were many alternatives for the continuance of operations. The experiences of the Allies' strategy hitherto made it easier for me to assess the probabilities.

The landing in Algiers could be considered almost a peacetime exercise; there had been no coastal defences to speak of. One could guess, with a probability nearing certainty, that the Allies would choose a task the success of which they could be confident, taking into consideration their limited training, especially in amphibious operations, and their strength. They attached great importance to powerful air cover, and this could not be provided from aircraft carriers alone. This meant the choice of an objective within easy striking distance of fighter aircraft operating from a fixed base.

These considerations ruled out the south of France, northern Italy and the Balkans (except an approach to them across the toe of Italy). Allied sea and air resources likewise pointed to Sicily, which could be successfully assaulted with the forces available and at the same time admitted the feasibility of a diversionary attack on south Calabria incidental to the main operation. It was not impossible that the enemy might bypass Sicily and launch his offensive in the direction of Sardinia and Corsica, enticed by the tempting bait of Rome as a long-range objective, but the imponderable difficulties made this unlikely.

The above appreciation of the situation is quoted by kind permission from Field-Marshal Kesselring's forthcoming memoirs entitled A Soldier's Testament.

Such were enemy thoughts in the spring of 1943.

How to muddle Hitler despite the advice of his professional strategists – that was the object of the next Allied Cover Plan. A mysterious and important operation in that plan took place in Spain. The finding of the master clue to our deception ten years afterwards, and the piecing together of the Cover Plan for the invasion of Sicily, is the subject of this book.

LIST OF ILLUSTRATIONS

*The following reproductions appear in a section from
pages 121–35 of the text.*

I

HOW THE QUEST BEGAN

This is the story of a quest for a corpse buried secretly in a strange place under a false name. You would think that a murder had been committed. Surprisingly it was His Majesty's Government that arranged the affair.

How was it that I came to be searching for that corpse, without knowing the rank or the name of the man, without even knowing where his grave was, or the date of his burial?

It was because the corpse was alleged to be the essential and inseparable part of an intelligence operation – the strangest intelligence operation, surely, of all time.

Intelligence as a subject has always interested me. It is sometimes more dramatic and often less real than journalism, in which the public demands hard facts and quick results. Intelligence has several dimensions. One of them is deception. Sometimes journalism brings you to the brink of that other world, the last dimension in which people move oddly, behave oddly, speak in whispers,

1

look over their shoulders and act as if life was one tremendous mystery. Meet those people, hear their intense subdued tones and you realise that you have walked into the remoter ends of the intelligence world. Back out while you can, because it is not your climate. Read about it – from a distance.

I had been spending some months investigating the strange behaviour of Admiral Wilhelm Canaris, the Chief of German Military Intelligence Services during the war. His elusive figure had appeared in foreign capitals, Berne, Madrid, and at fitful intervals Lisbon. Here and there he had dropped a meaningful hint, and here and there he had omitted some action that might have done us great harm, and often he had protected German agents abroad who were disloyal to the Führer. His was a curious career of contradictory actions.

'But he was never a British agent,' a Minister of the Crown frowned across his soup at me as we sat at dinner. 'Was he?'

'Hitler may have suspected him of being something of the kind,' I answered, 'in view of some leakages of military secrets. If not a British agent – then an enemy of Hitler.'

A little later the Cabinet Minister remarked thoughtfully: 'Yes, Canaris may have connived at a leakage, but some "leakages" are useful – like the one described in *Operation Heartbreak*.'

I pricked up my ears.

Operation Heartbreak, I recollected, was a novel, a book of the month, published in 1950 by the firm of Rupert Hart-Davis. In it the Rt. Hon. Sir Alfred Duff Cooper, now Viscount Norwich, related the pleasant and moving story of an officer whose dead body is put with false documents in a place where the enemy will discover them. It is the story of a masterstroke of deception, requiring the grim encumbrance of a human body.

Was that novel then founded on the fact? I endeavoured not to show surprise, lest the Minister should add those words that have so often knelled on the hopes of journalists – 'What I am telling you is off the record.'

But he did not do so, and that night I took down the novel and dipped into it again. Yes, there was a man's body, a man who failed in life and succeeded in death, and a girl friend who slipped a letter into his pocket before they floated him out on to a neutral coast carrying false strategic documents with him. There was an eerie suggestion of truth about the book, a mischievous reality.

Was there then really a body that had been used for this purpose? Who was the unknown soldier? Ought a former Cabinet Minister to borrow a plot for fiction from the secret bookshelves of Deception of the Enemy?

All these questions occurred to me. Later I heard that it had been thought in some circles that the novel had sailed close to the wind of official secrets.

The most intriguing question remained. Whose body? Beneath what unknown tomb?

Sir Alfred Duff Cooper described his hero as Captain William Maryngton, a pleasant softish regular officer, who had always failed to get to the front – until he was dead. Was it possible that this honour, the role of the unknown courier, was conferred upon some hospital casualty? What might have been the character of the man whose body had been used in this way? What would he have said about it all himself?

Further on in the novel there was a description of the boutique fantasque where these secret operations were planned, and a portrait of a gruff old intelligence officer who declared roundly that when they wanted bodies – as if that was a routine occurrence – they had to use the body of a lunatic tramp. But would that have been the truth in a case like this, in which the corpse must have the appearance of an officer? What a strange ending chapter to the life

3

of any man, and how much more strange if you could discover how his life began, who he was, and what accident of fate set him upon the last journey! With that in mind I ranged a little further in search of the character for this shadowy person.

If you have heard one detail of a case, be sure you will hear more within a day or so. I sat in a West End club and heard some details of the table talk that had hailed the little novel.

'Some people are saying that this novel about a body being sent ashore with false papers is quite true.'

To Mr Clement Attlee, then Prime Minister, this remark was gently directed by a young lady over the dinner table at Eton. Mr Attlee is too old a hand to be trapped by such innuendoes.

'Some trick of the kind is said to have been used in the First World War,' he fended.

It was not hard to find people in London who had heard the legend of the floating body with its forged documents. They told vague details of a faked aircraft accident, but nobody could give me his name, and nobody could say when he was tipped into the sea or where he was buried. So to all intents and purposes it remained a club story, part fiction, and it went to the back of my mind, to that remote lobe of the brain where a journalist stores occasional remarks that do not bear investigation.

There lodged my surmise about the hoax with a body for many months. I fancied at times that the case could be related to the invasion of Normandy in June 1944, an operation carefully prepared with all manner of strategic deception to keep Hitler guessing. To save thousands of lives, even that grim jest with a human body would have been justified. If it was not Normandy, the case must relate either to the landings in Sicily in July 1943, or to the first big combined landings of all, Operation 'Torch', in which Generals Eisenhower and Alexander caught and crushed the Afrika Korps on the North African coast. Obviously the floating corpse must have carried with it documents suggesting a landing elsewhere than was really intended. In that sense I read the intriguing little novel. In that direction such hints as I could gather all pointed.

I calculated also that with a little more detail, it would be gradually possible to reconstruct this fascinating stratagem. That the papers on the case might be released for publication I hardly expected. The Secret Services of this world do not care to demonstrate how clever they were. It is for the defeated enemy, the penurious and pensionless officers of the Wehrmacht to crow about their intelligence successes.

There was probably some detail close to the real thing in the novel that I had read, otherwise it would not have caused so much concern in official circles. I looked at the map of Europe during the war years. The puzzle was to find a neutral coast, on which the documents found with a floating corpse might readily become available to the German intelligence service. Only Portugal and Spain seemed to be likely, and on the whole I believed that it must have been on the Spanish coast. There could not be many graves of British officers in Spain. So my speculations roamed. Then they ceased.

I ceased to think about this mystery until one day I was standing on the kerb of St James's Street, when Julian hailed me.

'You remember your theory of the corpse that could never be published,' he said.

'Yes, what about it?'

'Do you know that there is a reference to something remarkably like it in a book by General Westphal – Kesselring's Chief of Staff?'

'Is it recognisable?' I asked.

Julian said: 'It's an extraordinary thing that so little notice has been taken of this admission – it seems to confirm the novel.'

'Then I shall be able to test my theory with a clear mind?'

'What is your theory?'

'That you can't hide a corpse. That corpses don't lie still.'

'Are you going to try and find him?'

'I will, if it is clear that such an investigation would no longer be – I am searching for a word.'

'Ill advised?'

'No, that's not the word.'

'No longer – reprehensible?' suggested Julian.

'That's it, that is just the word I was groping for. No longer reprehensible.'

'Well it's quite plain,' said Julian, 'that the body was carrying papers relating to the invasion of Sicily.'

'Not Normandy?'

'No, Sicily, and the German High Command was thinking about the corpse and its false intelligence in the middle of 1943. They didn't know where we would hit next.'

'So the operation and the burial of the unknown soldier, if he existed, took place in the months preceding our attack on Sicily.'

'That would be May or June in 1943,' suggested Julian.

We stood on the windy corner of St James's opposite Berry's wine shop and worked it out.

'Your body was an officer of the rank that would be entrusted with important dispatches,' said Julian. 'A Lieutenant-Commander, a Captain or a Major. Perhaps a Lieutenant-Colonel.'

I said: 'He was most probably "lost" and buried on the south or south-west coast of Spain. That is the way our communications ran to Gibraltar and Malta and all our war bases beyond. Our lines of communication would not touch the east or the north coasts of Spain.'

'I admire your reasoning,' said Julian. 'I hope it is right.'

'The date on his grave would be between February 1943, when

planning of the invasion of Sicily (Operation "Husky") started, and July when the attack was launched. And his body may well have been brought back to Gibraltar for burial,' I said confidently. 'I'll go and try to find him. I am grateful to you, Julian.'

'Spain is a large place,' said Julian. 'You'll have a job. Why not dig a bit here first? And in the meanwhile I'll let you know exactly what Westphal says.'

This was not bad advice. I went to the Spanish Embassy in Belgrave Square.

'Really you British are the most extraordinary people,' said the Spanish Attaché. 'Do you mean to say that when you attack a coast, you send swimming corpses in ahead of you, here and there?'

His fingers made an expressive wriggling movement towards an imaginary coastline.

'Oh no,' I said. 'I am speaking of one particular intelligence operation that is not likely to be repeated.'

'Then it is one body which you wish me to help in finding, one only?' said the Spanish Attaché. 'Well this is no ordinary request, but I will ask.'

'As he was a military messenger carrying war dispatches, perhaps you can find some trace of correspondence about him,' I suggested.

The Attaché nodded and asked me to return on the following day. I did so.

'By great good fortune,' said the Spaniard, 'I have met one of our diplomats who remembers this case, or a case something like it. A body was washed up near Tarifa in 1943, and I believe he is buried there. His papers would have been returned.'

Tarifa – I found it on the map near Gibraltar, a tiny fishing village. I rang up the War Graves Commission at High Wycombe and spoke to the principal archivist.

Could you help me trace a grave on the south coast of Spain? I am afraid I do not know the name, but some German memoirs refer to the body of a British military courier buried possibly at Tarifa in 1943, who was carrying dispatches and was drowned at sea. I want to ascertain whether the incident is actually true. If I give you the approximate dates, maybe you can find a grave that fits with the circumstances.

Did I merely fancy that the archivist was the least bit wary? It is seldom worthwhile to imagine things or to ponder on what is unsaid. I was after facts and his answer was factual enough after all.

Said the archivist: 'If the man whom you are looking for was a courier, then that is a matter for the Ministry of Defence. They may not want to tell you about a courier, but if they give you a name, we will gladly help you to trace the grave, if we have got him.'

That seemed fair enough, though when I thought of enquiring at the Ministry of Defence, it seemed to me unlikely that the austere Ministry would open its lips at the first approach.

I told an old friend, General Sir Frank Mason Macfarlane, what General Westphal had revealed. As he had been Governor of the Rock during 1943, it was not out of the question that if a corpse were floated ashore on the nearby coast, General Macfarlane might have known about it.

'As to all such questions, my answer is always the same – no comment,' said 'Mason-Mac'.

It would have been about as easy to have got an answer from the Rock of Gibraltar itself.

Besides, it seemed to me important to test my theory that the investigation of this intelligence operation must begin with the finding of the grave. That was the right approach. No doubt people in London knew something of the legendary corpse, learned during the course of their wartime duties, but to induce any one of them to discuss this operation would have seemed poor sport. Who would wish to shoot at a sitting bird? The story should come from the scene of action.

Wherever that was! The telephone rang. It was Julian on the line. He said: 'Here you are. I've got General Siegfried Westphal's book *The German Army in the West* in my hand. Have you a pencil and paper? I'm going to read from page 150.'

There was a footnote to page 150, concerning the war in Italy during 1943.

> The German High Command had to admit to being deceived by a clever enemy ruse. The body of a British courier had been washed ashore in Spain, and was found to be carrying documents concerning an impending landing by strong enemy forces in Greece. As a result, German divisions, including Panzer formations, were transferred with great difficulty to the Peloponnese.

I booked an air ticket to Gibraltar via Madrid, and drew my £25 travel allowance. The Spanish Embassy was most friendly about a visa.

'What makes you so sure about being able to reconstruct this operation?' asked Julian.

I said: 'In most intelligence stories, there are papers locked away somewhere. You apply to see the papers. You give some incredibly pompous reason for wanting to have access to them, and the Under Secretary of State writes you a letter in reply:

DEAR SIR,
I have to thank you for your application to examine the documents relevant to Operation 'Blimp'.

I regret to have to inform you that until they are released to the public these documents cannot be seen by any persons not of Her Majesty's Service.

I have the honour to be ... etc.'

'Yes,' said Julian. 'I know that kind of letter.'

'But in this case, there is a body,' I said, 'and somebody must own to him sooner or later, some regiment or service. That is why I'm after finding the body.'

I explained my theory to the Rev. Cyril Armitage, the vicar of St Bride's whom occasionally I meet at the Press Club. He is an old friend of war days when he was Chaplain to the Royal Marines, Plymouth Division.

The vicar, who in St Bride's vaults keeps the largest store of latifundia in the kingdom, agreed that a body, though difficult to find, is also difficult to hide.

'Bodies are fascinating things,' he said. 'Even dead bodies are interesting. I once preached a sermon on the difficulty of getting rid of a body, but you are in a hurry now. I'll tell you more about it when you get back.'

Finally I comforted myself with the thought that there is not, there cannot be, an Official Secrets Act upon the dead, even if they could tell tales.

I flew to Spain, to find the body, and if there was a body, to find out who he really was.

2

THE TRACES IN MADRID

'That will be ten shillings,' said the cashier at London air station. 'It used to be five shillings.'

'I know, sir.'

'And before that it was nothing at all.'

'I have awful difficulty in collecting it,' complained the official.

'What do I get for ten shillings?'

'There's the bus ride to the airport and services at the airports.'

I said: 'This is a shabby imposition. I hope they take it off before the Coronation visitors start to arrive.'

'I dislike collecting it, believe me,' said the man at the desk, as he handed me my change.

There were no free services that I could find at London airport either.

Along the coast of Biscay the Viking flew past France into Spain. Below lay the sunlit snows of the Pyrenees, the brown highroad to

Burgos and the brown torrents running out of the mountains. Beyond the bare contours of Spain's immense snow-powdered Sierras.

In Madrid I hoped to find a friendly Spanish official who would help me in my search for a missing grave. At the Hotel Galicia I learned that these were the days of fiesta, and that the days of fiesta, a long vista of them, stretched from December into January. The Ministries were closed, the officials were away on their holidays.

This was not a case of *mañana*, but of waiting until after the Feast of the Three Kings had been celebrated on 6 January, in the New Year of 1953.

I had arrived in Madrid on 28 December. I whiled away a leisure hour at the British Embassy chatting to the counsellor, Ralph Murray, an old friend. The keen wintry sunlight hit the dome of San Francesco's cathedral and glowed in the brick patios. The crowds trailed through the Avenue Jose Antonio, shop gazing. The urchins ran about offering fountain pens for sale and tripping you up with shoe shine boxes. Time was not on my side. If the Spaniards were away, and the British knew nothing, I must turn to the Germans.

The Germans in Madrid are a useful colony when it comes to summoning up remembrance of things past. They have much time to ponder. I write it to the credit side of the Spaniards that they did not, like some other countries when the Third Reich collapsed, ungratefully eject all German citizens as undesirable. Spain was not intimidated. She gave refuge to some and the promise of work to others. A few of the doormen at the hotels are Germans, and there are German translators, technicians and business men. True that other less welcome guests, former members of the Gestapo and the German security services, have filtered back into Spain and managed to get a foothold again. The German colony in Madrid is large and informative. It includes Alois Miedl, Hitler's picture fancier, though he took Dutch nationality some years ago; it includes, of course, Skorzeny, the strong-arm man with his business agency; it includes gentle, reticent people like Joacquim Canaris, the nephew of the famous admiral, and on the fringe of this community in touch with all their movements stands Rudolf the Good.

Rudolf is an Austrian. As such he saw the error of Hitler's ways quite soon and chose freedom while the war was still being fought. Rudolf can therefore afford a lofty attitude towards some of his more benighted fellow Germans. He runs with them rather like a sheep-dog, remembers all their faces, counts them daily, knows where they are. A telephone call to Rudy brought him round to my hotel to have a cup of coffee, sitting on the crimson velvet settees of the lounge.

'Ach,' said Rudolf nodding around him, 'you are back here in your old diggings, looking for something more about Admiral Canaris.'

'Rudolf, I would like to meet one or two of the German intelligence officers who used to operate on the south coast of Spain during the war. Some of them will certainly have retired to Madrid.'

'That is just so,' said Rudolf. 'There is Fritz Baumann, the frog-man officer. Just mention my name to him.'

'Is not Captain Wilhelm Lenz in town, the former senior officer of Admiral Canaris in Spain?' I asked.

'Yes, of course I know him,' said Rudolf. 'He too is here.'

I said that I had come to do some research about a war grave, so the talk turned to cemeteries.

'The English cemeteries of Spain,' said Rudolf,

are something for which all nations must be grateful. During the war Germans and other enemy nationalities were buried in the English cemeteries. Except for the Roman Catholics, there is no place in Spanish cemeteries for us.

Look in Madrid cemetery. You will find Austrians, Jews,

Americans, Germans, French, British, Russians all together, and a few whose true religion is not known find their way to the English cemetery. The British vice-consuls and the British chaplain have many to look after here in Spain.

Rudolf the Good drank up his coffee and left me there, and I rang up Captain Wilhelm Lenz at his flat in the Avenue Habana. Captain Lenz accepted an invitation to dinner.

He came punctually, a short white-haired man with a birdlike brightness of eye. From the first he gave more the impression of a diplomat than an intelligence officer. He was quiet, soft spoken, respectable.

Obviously he had spent many years receiving his daily quota of intelligence reports from Spanish Headquarters in Madrid. Obviously, too, this elderly gentleman had never been an ardent Nazi, and obviously Canaris had known as much when he left Lenz as his senior officer in Spain during the war.

The waiter brought us small lobsters, a south coast delicacy, and dry sherry.

'You are the first Englishman that I have met since the war,' said Captain Lenz. 'It would interest me therefore to compare notes with you. I returned to Germany at the end of the war, and spent some months in internment camp. When I was eventually released, General Vigon, who is now Chief of Spanish Army General Staff, was good enough to permit me to return here.'

The old man sipped his pale sherry and looked out across the Calle Antonio Primo de Rivera.

'Once,' he said,

I missed what you journalists would call a scoop. Is not that the word? I employed a young lady to sit about these cafes and listen to what Allied visitors might be discussing. In December 1942, she overheard some American airman talking about an important meeting of the Allied statesmen, Mr Churchill and President Roosevelt, at Casablanca.

Now we could not quite believe that these officers would talk so openly about a conference so near at hand. So I worked out that Casablanca must be a code word for 'White House' and that they would meet in Washington. Within a week or so the meeting took place at Casablanca. Sometimes the simplest explanation is the best.

Then he told me of the crucial meeting between General Franco and Admiral Canaris in January 1940, when Hitler sent his Chief of Intelligence to ask for passage through Spain to attack Gibraltar.

Captain Wilhelm 'Lenz' (the name under which he operated)
Senior German Intelligence Officer in Spain 1936–1945

Canaris said not a word throughout the whole meeting after delivering his message. It was a long monologue by Franco.

As we drove back to Madrid from Franco's residence, the admiral turned to me and asked: 'Now what was it that the Caudillo was saying?'

I answered: 'The sense of that long speech in one word was No!'

Canaris sank back on the cushions of the car with a look of relief. He did not relish the idea of an advance through Spain to attack Gibraltar.

We sat and drank another sherry.

'There is one incident I should like to ask you about,' said Lenz as he cracked the lobster claws in nut crackers. 'I recollect that there was an interesting collection of documents found during the war on the body of a British courier who was drowned off the south coast of Spain.'

This was highly interesting to me.

'I believe I know which case you mean, Captain Lenz.'

'The documents were important. I eventually saw photostats of them.'

'Have you kept copies of them?'

'No, I destroyed my files at the end of the war.'

'Indeed, what a pity! Are you sure there was a body?'

'I received a report from my agent in the south.'

'Cannot you remember where this British courier was buried?'

'It was somewhere within the Seville command area. I cannot remember where. The report came to me, I think, from my agent in Cadiz. I cannot even remember the agent's name. It is many years ago, and I have heard it suggested that the whole incident was a "plant" to deceive us.'

'Then there may have been no body at all?'

'I do not know. I can only remember what my agent reported at the time. He said that the drowned body of a high British officer had been washed up in the Seville command carrying important papers. It would interest me to know from you whether this was really so.'

'I am myself interested in just this case,' I replied. 'I am going south to find out whether there is really a grave.'

'I recollect that the documents referred to the operations in the Mediterranean in the summer of 1943,' pursued Lenz. 'There had been an aircraft accident.'

This was indeed fortunate. I had not even broached the subject. Lenz had started to speak of it himself. Evidently the incident was still puzzling him after ten years.

'I will enquire at the Spanish General Staff,' pursued Lenz, 'whether they have any records left. When you return to Madrid, if you are coming back this way, maybe I shall be able to tell you more, when I have refreshed my memory with Spanish friends here who remember the case.'

After Lenz there was Joacquim Canaris to see but the nephew of Admiral Canaris could not recollect anything. So I telephoned to Major Fritz Baumann.

Major Fritz Baumann was one of the names under which he operated, and he has asked me to use this name in my narrative.

He appeared in my hotel, a towering man, broad in proportion, with shaggy brown hair and keen brown eyes in a tanned complexion. He stood for a while, stiff, hesitant, not quite rid of his military manner, and wondering what it was that I wanted of him.

'I am doing historical research on the war on the fringes of Spain,' I said. 'Perhaps you can help me.'

Baumann sat down and talked about his work. He had been enlisted at the outbreak of war in 1939 from the German police in the rank of a Major of the German Army. After two years he had been seconded to the Abwehr or Intelligence Service and had been posted to Spain in the autumn of 1942 as an officer of Abwehr II, the sabotage branch. As such he had trained and led small commandos of Spaniards in the technique of frogmen, to attack British warships in Gibraltar and British merchant ships in Seville and Huelva with limpet time-bombs.

I should think he was a competent frogman leader ten years ago: no man to meet bathing by moonlight; intrepid and ruthless in carrying out his orders.

'I used to operate from Madrid,' said Fritz, 'making sudden sorties onto the south coast. I knew the Algeciras branch of our Intelligence Service, who used to watch your shipping at Gibraltar; the Seville branch, the Cadiz and the Huelva agents, who specialised in reports on your merchant shipping. There was the yearly Seville orange crop which was loaded at the wharves of Seville. Well, there was often a bomb of mine in those crates. Our object in setting the time fuses was to produce an explosion at sea, so that it would seem to have been a submarine attack.'

I could not forbear, as I thought of the orange hold after an explosion, to murmur with de Maupassant 'Quelle marmalade!'

'Well, after a time the British got wise to those tricks, and they froze a cargo on the quayside, so that the next bomb exploded in Seville docks. The Spaniards were not pleased at that, so we started to attach our bombs with magnets to the bottoms of the ships. One British crew in the Rio Tinto saw one of these bombs from a boat and were bold enough to detach it. After that I had to build in a secondary contact fuse. We were never at the end of our ruses.'

'And counter-ruses?'

Yes, as you say. Of course the Rio Tinto shipping was much more important than the oranges, because the Rio Tinto mines provide you with copper and pyrites for your munitions.

I attacked the shipping at Gibraltar too, but that I did by bribing the dockyard labourers who go daily from the mainland to Gibraltar. I used to rent a back room in Algeciras, never registering with the police, and brief my men there. With my field glasses from a roof or through the telescope on the Abwehr villa, we could watch for results across the bay.

The finest exploit against Gibraltar, however, was that of the Italians who had a merchant ship trapped in Algeciras alongside the quay. It could not run the gauntlet of the British Navy, and so it was immobilised. The Italians stealthily brought in bits of machinery in small consignments and built a submersion chamber into the hull below the waterline. They brought in their human torpedoes in parts from Italy via the South of France and the Pyrenean frontier. They assembled them below decks and launched them from a man-size torpedo vent by night and went in to attack your shipping in the roads, steering the torpedoes astride midget motor boats.

Well, as the war went on, I moved north with it. I led my frogmen in commando attacks on British bridges across rivers behind the Allied lines. Then came defeat, then came internment, and as I was an intelligence officer and a special operator, I can tell you that internment was not pleasant at times.

'Were you beaten up?'

'I have nothing to say about that.'

'You know, Fritz, that internment for those who lose a war can never be pleasant. Yet it could hardly have been worse for you than it was for those agents of ours whom the Gestapo was wiping out before the final surrender – the noose, the gas chamber, the furnace if they were in a hurry, and not always unconscious when the body went in.'

'I'm not complaining,' said Fritz. 'We lost.'

'I made an attempt to visit the Allied internment camps in 1946,' I said, 'but it was not permitted.'

'What I didn't like was the degradation,' said Fritz. 'Then afterwards I had a chance of lively work in Europe. No, thank you! A quiet job for me!'

'What was your job before the war?' I asked.

'I was a police pathologist,' said Fritz.

'A what?'

'I used to specialise on corpses.'

'On corpses?'

'Yes, particularly on drowned corpses, or shall we say on corpses recovered from water, because you can never be sure until you have held an autopsy whether a body died from immersion, or whether it was thrown into the water afterwards.'

'That was your profession?'

'I studied first in law, and then in the forensic branch of Hamburg Police Academy. Does this interest you? As I became specialised I saw and examined hundreds of corpses. I learned to detect whether wounds were self-inflicted, whether decomposition had taken place on shore or in the water, whether a man had tied a weight round his own neck in committing suicide, or whether he was thrown in dead. You can pretty well tell from the lungs and the larynx whether a man has died of drowning. I even made a study of rat bites as compared to fish bites on corpses.'

'What did you do in the war before they sent you to Spain?'

'When I was enlisted,' said Fritz Baumann, 'I was put on to studying the human injuries involved in aircraft accidents. I have examined the bodies of scores of airmen killed both on land and at sea. I have made long reports on the causes of death and the extent of injuries. My knowledge as a pathologist was most useful.'

So at about the time that the British secret planning staff was devising how to fake an air accident and float a corpse ashore as if it had really drowned there, here was a German officer posted to the spot who would be probably better fitted than any other man on the continent to detect the fraud.

South-coast Fritz apologised for boring me with so much detail.

'Do you remember the case of the drowned British courier?' I asked him.

'Yes indeed I do,' said Fritz.

It intrigued me when I heard about it, because I have a professional interest in bodies.

I remember that reports about it came from the Seville area. The description was of a corpse with a despatch case fastened to its waist with a chain. That seemed to me to correspond with the British habit for carrying important dispatches. I have sometimes travelled in the same airliner as those couriers. They would not have known me, of course.

So I asked a few questions in the Seville District H.Q. about the case. It struck me that the Spaniards were most reticent about the documents, whereas usually it was not difficult to find things out at the Headquarters of the Captain-General of the Seville command. That made me think that it was important.

'What about the body? Do you know where that was buried?'

'It may have been at Cadiz. I do not know.'

So Dr Fritz Baumann had brought his specialised knowledge all the way from Hamburg to Seville without applying it to the case. He had gone after the documents. He had not gone after the body. Now, however, he was beginning to think about that body.

'Tell me then,' he said. 'Do you know where the body was buried?'

'Not yet. I hope to find out when I go to Gibraltar.'

'It would certainly have interested me to have seen the body,' said Fritz. Something was dawning on him and he scanned my face for another clue to my thoughts.

'It was an aircraft accident, was it not?' said he. 'Yes that would have interested me too – to know whether he was killed or drowned. If an aircraft crashes into the sea, they don't often get out.'

It was New Year's Eve. Why should I spoil the frogman's holiday? I told him that I hoped to see him when I had finished my research in Andalusia. Outside the singing, shouting crowd moved slowly up and down the avenue. The Spaniards were clasping the twelve grapes that they swallow one by one as the strokes of midnight sound. In the cafes they were hotly arguing whether the bull's horn tips should be sawn off, as the practice has been in recent years. This was not improving the performance of the bull or the bull-fighter, it was slowing down the bull and giving the matador more scope for elegance in his passes. For the operation severed certain nerves and impaired the bull's sense of direction. If it was not that in Madrid that they discussed as the old year closed, then it was the parting between Rosario and Antonio. They had danced for years together, and he, the entrancing figure with the faience manner, had often outdanced her. Something in her vibrant temperament turned inimical to him in the end, and they had quarrelled. She and the quiet solemn guitarist remained together. Antonio declared that he would turn to ballet. This was the talk of Madrid above all else, the talk of the cafés verging on the broad avenues of wintry sunlight, and much more to be discussed than the sterile question of bases for America. Certainly of far greater moment, the quarrel of Rosario with Antonio, than the whereabouts of a nameless corpse in an unknown grave.

3

THE ROCK OF GIBRALTAR

The Rock lay dominant on the Spanish coast, as the aircraft made a slow sweep over the Straits. And as the lights of the town went up, glimmering round its nether slope, there lay the Moorish giant that the Dons had captured after five hundred years, and that a quarter of a millennium later the British had captured from the Dons.

On either side of the Rock, the immense bare coast stretched away towards Malaga to the east and Cadiz to the west.

The runway has been extended out to sea across the neck of the isthmus, where the airport has replaced the racecourse. In the untidy customs shed a Gibraltar customs officer explained to me the intricacies of the exchange regulations between the Gibraltar pound and the peseta, and then we drove out of the neutral zone through a gate in the casemates into the long, narrow main street that is Gibraltar. It was with a homely feeling of pride that I saw the same domed helmets as London policemen wear. The hotel in the town was stone flagged, bare and dreary. A naval officer and his wife were quarrelling in the room next to mine. There is a shortage of married quarters in Gibraltar, and what naval officer can afford the Rock Hotel's prices? Poor naval wives!

Across the Straits in French Morocco, round the new American air base, the trim modern married quarters were going up with the nearby glories of the Post Exchange store.

All the same, I, for one, would not exchange the crowded honours of old Gibraltar for any modernity. Past the Convent, the Governor's residence with its orange trees glowing in the patio, I climbed to the Garrison Library and the *Gibraltar Chronicle* offices to make some enquiries.

That morning I had started early as the first sun at breakfast time made the shopkeepers lift their shutters, and walked round the cemeteries of Gibraltar.

Gibraltar has two cemeteries, and these I searched by the thin clear light of early morning – one was the Trafalgar cemetery, an old churchyard of grey headstones in the town itself, where nobody had been buried for many years. He was not likely to be there. Walking northward towards the neutral zone, there lay beside the airport and under the immense limestone bluff of the Rock the main cemetery of Gibraltar.

Those who have toured the livelier places of foreign countries would do well to spend an hour or so in such a cemetery. It brings tranquillity, irons out the bustle of life, puts our worries into proportion.

> I would rather stay
> With tombs than cradles to wear out a day.

Acacia, mimosa and palm grew there. Over the tombs flourished clover in plenty. Here were tombs with Spanish names and with British names. Two Bishops of Gibraltar share this cemetery for the Anglican and the Roman faith. There are many inscriptions in English. One of these tombs the illiterate Spanish gravediggers had laid facing inwards over an elderly Englishman so that his name could hardly be read from the path. On through knobs, obelisks and railings I reached the plain white crosses of the Second World War, several hundred in number, and began to tell them by date. I was looking for a cross that bore the dates between March and June 1943. In those months, I calculated, the incident would have been placed.

The cemetery keeper shuffled up with a tactful mournful eye, as if he expected me to make some enquiry of him. As I did not, he passed on among the tombs.

There was no officer's cross among the brotherhood of the dead that fitted with the facts as I had been told them. So he had not been brought in to Gibraltar, unless, unless he had been buried here under his real name and perhaps with no rank – for the legend was that alive he had never really been an officer. There was no reason to suppose that the deception had been kept up for ever, especially when the Sicily operation was over – and yet, it must have been necessary to bury him quickly, and once buried, a corpse likes to lie where it is and not change its name. So I argued with the headstones.

It was with a pang that in searching on from one row to another I came upon the grave of an old friend, Colonel Victor Cazalet, whom I had last seen at Swift's stooking his corn, open shirted and exuberant, reciting Keats's ode to autumn as he worked. Cazalet had died here at Gibraltar on 4 July 1943, with General Sikorski, the Polish national leader, to whom he acted as wartime liaison officer. Their aircraft, piloted by a Pole, had taken off by night from the Gibraltar runway and plunged steeply into the sea. With them perished Sikorski's daughter and Brigadier Whiteley. The Rock had first heard the news from a BBC announcement several days later. Sikorski was not here, his body having been taken back to England in a destroyer. This much I remembered.

There was no separate plot for officers; all lay side by side, the Rear-Admiral next to the rating. At an odd angle under an acacia tree apart from the rest was one grave that I eyed long and thoughtfully, that of Allan Mian, merchant seaman, buried 17 September 1943; but none of these inscriptions helped me in my search. I walked back into Gibraltar town, reflecting that perhaps he had not been brought in at all, that perhaps the War Graves Commission's policy in this hot climate was not to gather in their dead. Perhaps he was still at Tarifa or Cadiz, or wherever he was first interred as he came out of the sea.

Or had he been buried at sea? But that would have removed his value as evidence that there had been such an incident.

Up the long street of Gibraltar to the Garrison Library and the office of the *Gibraltar Chronicle*, and there I found its editor, the Garrison librarian, Mr E. F. Ryan. I told him something of my research.

'I don't remember anything like that ever being reported,' said Ryan. 'There was one case of a Catalina aircraft that sank in the Straits and two bodies washed up; something about a loss of a secret courier is mentioned in Sir Samuel Hoare's book *Ambassador on Special Mission*. Would you like to refer to it?'

He kindly installed me in the roomy old library with a copy of the book of the present Lord Templewood.

Sir Samuel Hoare had written this book very soon after the war; it was turned out in a piquant and racy style that was more reminiscent of my profession than his, and it very nearly succeeded in proving that it was Sir Samuel and not the American Ambassador in Madrid, Mr Hayes, who kept Spain out of the war to the great detriment of Hitler's cause. Tearing myself away from the glowing portrait that Sir Samuel painted of the wicked foreign minister, Ramon Serrano Suner, I found the passage about the incident with the papers.

'There were moments of extreme anxiety,' he wrote of the weeks in autumn 1942 immediately preceding Operation 'Torch'.

> The worst was after my return to Madrid, when my excellent military and naval attachés gave me some very disturbing news. The body had been washed ashore near Cadiz of a naval officer who was carrying from General Clark to the Governor of Gibraltar the final details of the 'Torch' landings. Further enquiries confirmed that the body was in the hands of the Spanish naval authorities. All that was possible was to ask that it be handed over to us and hope that the secret papers had not been discovered. The Ministry of Marine, always better disposed to us than the Ministry of War, agreed to our request and when the dead officer's effects were examined, there was no evidence of any tampering with the papers. None the less, the doubt remained as to whether they had not been read and re-sealed, a doubt that persisted until 'Torch' actually started. In the meantime the ingenious minds in London were more than ever active laying false trails, one of which in particular took the enemy hounds galloping off to Italy and the Far East.

I laid down Sir Samuel's book more perplexed than when I took it up. Here indeed was such an incident as General Westphal and Mr Duff Cooper had described in their respective works with some differences in detail. If the British Ambassador had not been let into the secret, this could be the same incident. But the Westphal note apparently spoke of the courier as floating ashore in the summer of 1943, whereas Sir Samuel was plainly referring to the autumn of 1942. What could be the true version? I remembered the Spanish Attaché in London wriggling his fingers. There could not have been dead couriers washed ashore before every operation.

But the bar of the Rock Hotel tended to confirm that there had been two bodies – and secret papers galore, and it had happened before Operation 'Torch' in 1942, not in 1943. So Westphal was wrong? Well, hardly!

I thought of a visit to Tarifa graveyard, and asked Jimmy the barman about Tarifa.

'Don't go there,' said Jimmy, 'it is only a fishing village. There is nothing at Tarifa to see, nothing at all.'

'Is there a cemetery?'

Jimmy shook a cocktail.

'That's about all.'

Some said the bodies had been buried at Tarifa, some mentioned Chiclana, others Cadiz, and even Jerez. At any rate they comforted me with the assurance that drowned bodies are buried the same day as they are washed up on the south coast of Spain. This seemed to confine my search to the coastal cemeteries of the Seville command, and although it is two hundred miles from the Rock to the frontier of Portugal, there are few towns and villages on the lonely Trafalgar coast, and one stretch of fifty miles is marshes only, Las Marismas beyond San Lucar, where the wild camels roam – the last living vestige of the Moorish invasion.

There was lunch at the Ryans' of fried swordfish, in the comfortable little house behind the Library. A shower fell, and the Ryan family were glad at the rain, for every drop that falls on the catchments of arid Gibraltar is precious to the water tanks. We ate our swordfish, neatly sliced and fried in batter, and afterwards I went for a walk to collect my thoughts. Up the winding Rock road till it met the sentinel's wall built by Charles V to hold off seaward pirates. The Rock lilies, wild narcissi, were out under the olive trees. Across the bay lay Algeciras, the observation base of the Germans in wartime.

That evening at the Rock bar there was an American communications officer who had arrived from North Africa to see which new base would suit him and his family.

'I think I am right in saying,' he explained, drawing a map with his finger on the bar top, 'that the coast of France at one point comes down to the Mediterranean up at the top of Spain. There's a port to see up there, is it Cadiz or Barcelona, and that is where I may be stationed.'

At the time of writing, there are still no American bases in Spain, and Gibraltar is of no great use to them, since its airport is too small, and there is no railhead.

The Rock Hotel people asked sympathetically whether I had found the grave.

Someone said: 'Why not go up to Jerez and see Guy Williams, the Vice-Consul. He is a partner in the firm of Humbert and Williams, and he will show you the famous sherry bodega. He knows a story of a Catalina aircraft that exploded between the Cape of Trafalgar and Cadiz during the war, and the bodies were washed ashore near his villa, with secret documents littered all over the beach.'

'But before you go,' they said, 'be sure to read up the battle of Barrosa, as it was near the Williams's villa that General Graham fought Marshall Victor in 1811 and captured the first French eagle of the Peninsular war.'

Yes, General Graham had taken part of the garrison of Cadiz by sea to Algeciras, and under a Spanish commander had marched back to attack the French forces besieging Cadiz. At Barrosa, as only the British can boast of doing, they had won great glory by attacking uphill against a more numerous French Army to recapture a ridge that they should never have left in the first place. With this knowledge of the battle of Barrosa, I prepared to call on the British Vice-Consul at Jerez. It was then that George offered to accompany me.

George I have known for some years now. He turns up with his twirled moustache and peaked cap, driving an uncomfortable open sports car at great speed. He is usually seeking the sun about this time of year with an elastic £25 and a blonde friend with a scarf tied over her head. This time she was not there and George was bored.

'I'll drive you to Jerez,' he said. 'We can taste the sherry and pump the Consul, and when you've found your body, we can bash on to Seville and see the flamenca girls in the Bodega of the Hotel Cristina.'

I thanked George for his kindness, and next day we slipped out of Gibraltar quite early; it was eleven o'clock on a quiet Sunday morning. After going through the Spanish customs at La Linea we would drive round the coast road westwards to Algeciras and Cadiz.

'I am fascinated by your theory,' said George. 'I can just imagine the British agent skulking round the Vice-Consul's villa waiting for the body to float in.'

'But what if some faithful retainer dashed down the beach and retrieved the package before the Spaniards had seen it,' I suggested. 'I don't see any advantage in floating in your body near the British Vice-Consul's villa, if you want to be sure that the Spaniards, or the Germans, get the papers.'

The Spanish customs at La Linea gave us clearance. We had now to follow the coastal road to Algeciras, then on to Tarifa, Chiclana and Cadiz, or inland to Jerez. We were following the route taken by General Graham's redcoats, and Hannibal before him.

Outside La Linea, there are hideous slums of huts built by the wandering Spanish labour that has been attracted to the Gibraltar dockyard or to the tobacco factory, a problem for the Spanish authorities, since the housing programme, if there is one, has been quite upset by this southward migration.

Behind us the Rock lay, its grim length, its wrinkled catchment slopes of concrete bleaching in the sun. One warship only lay in the harbour, and there had not been more stationed there for a long time. The high-prowed car ferry was running into the bay from Tangier, the local ferry was creeping between Gib and Algeciras. The wealth and the economic pull of the Rock, its magnetic effect on the coast around it, are hard to describe. I reflected that next year, 1954, would be the 250th year of British rule, and that it would be worth celebrating in royal style.

As we drove round the bay to Algeciras, George pointed out the estate of Count Ribetera, an Austrian by birth, the agent here of the Marquis of Bute, who owns the Rock Hotel.

'Ribetera was on meeting terms with the German Chief of Intelligence, Admiral Canaris,' said George. 'So they say on the Rock.'

Such are the international links that lie about still in southern Spain.

As we drove, I counted over the investigations that I had already made from Gibraltar by telephoning to Vice-Consuls. At Algeciras the records had no British officers buried, only a private and a sergeant. At Zaharas there was an able seaman. To my telephone enquiry the Consul at Cadiz, after consulting his registry of graves, had answered that there were no graves at all of British officers who had died in 1943. If all these records were correct, that narrowed our search. Oddly enough, there was no officer buried at Tarifa either, according to Consular records. So our hopes were set upon Chiclana, Jerez, and the little port of San Lucar. Beyond that, the marsh cut the coastal road and deflected it northwards to Seville.

We stopped in Algeciras at the Hotel Reina Maria Cristina, the mainland rival to the Rock Hotel – certainly its peer among luxury hotels. This hotel too is owned by Englishmen, and it has much to recommend it. Firstly, it is more moderate in its prices, and its orange and palm gardens above the sea beckon you again. The dignified hall porter, with his blue livery and snowy jabot below a vintage complexion, sent off to fetch the manager, and gravely, like an old nobleman, he watched us with melancholy pale-blue eyes. Lieb, the Austrian manager, and his English wife must have had an exciting time at Algeciras during the war with the spies of Canaris and Kaltenbrunner all over the place.

'We called them the glass eyes and the wooden eyes,' said Lieb. 'The Canaris men didn't see much, and the Gestapo men saw nothing at all.'

At the magical name of Canaris, one of the Spanish barmen went out for a breath of fresh air.

In my quest for the body of the nameless courier, there was not a clue in Algeciras – only light talk and pale sherry. We drove on.

George drove off at speed towards Vejer de la Frontera, past the dry lagoon of La Janda where the invading Moors routed the Visigoths in 711 and began their seven hundred years of domination in Spain. We lunched on mutton and beans with red wine at Vejer, and that, with our delay at Algeciras, left us short of time.

We could see the pinewoods and the sharp ridge of Barrosa that had caught Graham's eye as the only tactical feature of the coastline.

In Chiclana, squat and rather squalid, a Spanish policeman with a white helmet and blue chin grinned and offered to help us. He took pencilled notes and left his beat to make an inspection of the cemetery. Meanwhile the village idiot of Chiclana offered to pilot our car to the villa at Barrosa, and he stubbornly fought off the rival claims of nimbler boys to mount our car and guide us. Though everybody laughed at us passing, he gibbered us well along the right road to Barrosa, until we came to the villa. The Vice-Consul was not at home, but his gardener showed us the battle relics and then went on to tell us of the day that the bodies had been washed up on the beach.

Yes, there had been two bodies, and he had heard the aircraft droning round as if with engine trouble. There had been a dull explosion out to sea. Two bodies had been washed ashore a week later. They had been laid out in the Spanish tunny-canning factory west of the villa. He could not remember which month it had been – perhaps October, perhaps November – or which year.

It seemed too realistic for the incident that I was after. We bumped our way back to Chiclana, and dropped off the grinning loon. Our policeman shook his head. There was no British officer there in Chiclana cemetery that he could find.

He drank a sherry with us at a workman's bar, then took up his beat by the bridge again, cheerful and unshaven in his blue serge and a shiny white helmet, promising to inspect Chiclana cemetery and report on it whenever we wanted.

The main road took us in a skirting sweep past Cadiz and across the salt flats towards Jerez. Salt cairns shone white at intervals above the salt pans.

We drove into Jerez and were kindly asked in for a late tea at the Vice-Consul's house, a cool white mansion in the quiet and palmy streets of Jerez, adorned with polished wrought-iron inner doors to a delightful cool hall. Guy Williams, the British Consul and sherry exporter, is a somewhat bald man of senatorial appearance. At tea he told us the story of the Catalina aircraft and the bodies on the beach, which I have since been able to amplify.

It had been not quite as Sir Samuel Hoare had suggested, but the dates had indeed been in mid-November 1942, in the early stages of Operation 'Torch'. A Catalina aircraft was reported overdue between England and Gibraltar, and within earshot of Cadiz. It had been in difficulties of some kind. Then an explosion had destroyed it or sent it plunging to the bottom of the sea. The wreck was never found.

Soon cryptic messages reached Gibraltar from London asking for confirmation of the safe arrival of a Catalina aircraft of Coastal Command; but as it had not been signalled as leaving England for some reasons of security, Gibraltar was mystified. In London there was soon high concern, as the aircraft had carried officers with most secret copies of Operational Orders for 'Torch', intended for the Governor of Gibraltar, General Sir F. N. Mason-Macfarlane.

Worse was to follow. Within a few days, two bodies were washed up on the beach, an officer and a Foreign Office man, and with them a quantity of documents. The Spaniards from the neighbouring tunny factory carried in the bodies from the beach and collected the papers that were strewn about. The manager of the canning factory then telephoned to the Rock and asked for an officer to come and fetch the bodies.

A British officer was sent at once with a military truck to fetch the bodies, and when he had seen them loaded into his vehicle:

'And what about the papers?' asked the Spaniards.

He replied that he had received no instructions about that. He was only to fetch the bodies. So he left the canning factory with all haste for Gibraltar.

The Spaniards picked over the sodden documents doubtfully with some interest. Although their meaning was not at once clear to them, it was evident that the British had devoted immense care to compiling these documents. Especially intriguing were several thick lists of names – 'black lists, I supposed,' the manager of the factory told the British Consul afterwards. Actually these were most secret lists of de Gaulle's special agents in North Africa, upon whose cooperation much of the success of Operation 'Torch' was depending.

When the bodies were examined in Gibraltar, it was discovered with consternation that a most secret document with its envelope flap open was protruding from the pocket of one of the bodies. A second officer was dispatched along the coast road from Gibraltar to Cadiz with even greater haste than the first; but the German Abwehr agent in Cadiz was much closer to the scene than the garrison of Gibraltar.

This disturbing news reached London about the same time as it was discovered that another set of these same secret 'Torch' orders had been found lying loose on a Highgate street. An officer of the R.A.F.V.R. had taken them home to read at leisure and dropped them without noticing his loss. An old lady had found them on the pavement, shown them to her son, who had not liked the look of them and sent her with them to a police station.

When the Prime Minister had heard of the accident to the Catalina and the sequel in the tunny-canning factory near Barrosa, he had said, so the Consul related, that if God so willed that the Germans should learn about Operation 'Torch', there were now two ways in which they might do so. But he cancelled nothing. All went according to plan, and apparently the Germans, though they had known of the aircraft accident, did not know about the flotsam papers.

Such was the Consul's story. The evidence is conclusive that the Germans learned nothing. Nor had they guessed right about 'Torch'! When the German General Staff came to make its appreciation of the destination of the large convoy assembled at Gibraltar and the even larger Allied fleets moving eastwards through the Straits, it preferred to think that they were destined for the Eastern Mediterranean.

'Von Stohrer [the German Ambassador] was certainly out of luck,' wrote Sir Samuel Hoare.

> An officer of the Spanish naval staff insisted that the Allied expedition was destined for North Africa. The Ambassador scouted the idea and declared that he had the best possible information that the objectives were Italy and the Eastern Mediterranean … All German intelligence organisations in Spain were unanimous against the idea of an African invasion.

What had happened then? The German intelligence men in Spain, all too reliant on their Spanish sources of information, had sat and allowed themselves to be fed with intelligence reports. But much had happened in the middle two years of the war. The Allies had grown stronger, the Germans had begun to weaken themselves in Russia, the Allied intelligence services had begun to grow more robust, and the mysterious Canaris had held down the soft pedal on his intelligence organisation in Spain.

Gradually the Germans had begun to imbibe, without knowing it, deception material prepared for them by the British intelligence services. So despite the bodies on the beach of Barrosa there *was* no loss of security in Operation 'Torch'.

We drank our tea and pondered on this story.

'But wasn't there another man – a third man with documents – at some other time?'

I asked the Consul this in perplexity: there was something awry in my calculations. His story was not at all what I had expected. And he shook his head.

'I don't know of one,' he said as he took us down to our car.

George stopped the car at the English cemetery of Jerez. 'Let's just make sure he is not here,' he said.

If I should die in Spain it is at Jerez in Andalusia that I should like to be buried. This walled garden with its palms, its mimosa trees, its acacia and briars is the loveliest that I have ever seen. The venerable sherry merchants and Vice-Consuls lie there under their grey tombs. The sunlight gilds the orange groves of Jerez. Here and there the tombs of a Victorian gentleman travelling in Spain, who was unwise enough to drink water in the nineteenth century, lies among the English colony of the sherry country. Outside the garden where the patricians sleep, there is a shaded plot for the unfortu-nates of this world – unhappy lovers and renegades, whom Mother Church will not have. These draw towards the heretical English and are huddled in near them, not quite in the same grandeur indeed, but at any rate in good English company.

We started the car again at the English cemetery gate. 'He won't be in there,' I thought, as we passed the large Spanish cemetery.

'You can cross Jerez off your map now,' said George. 'That leaves you the coast south and east of Seville all the way to Portugal.'

'I am worried by the Vice-Consul's story,' I said.

'It seems so like the operation I suspect, and yet it is quite the opposite – wrong dates, two bodies and genuine papers.'

'Perhaps Don Guido felt he could not tell you the other story.'

'He'd have to be very deep for that,' said I. 'Perhaps rather he wouldn't know. After all it is not a Consul's job to get mixed up in secret operations with bodies, and then the body may not have been washed up in his area.'

'Wait till we get to Seville,' said George. 'There is a Consul-General there. You can take a look in the Graves Register for the whole area of the Consulate-General. That will cover the same area as the Seville command, so if these papers that you talk about fin-ished up at Seville H.Q., the third man must be buried within the Seville area.'

'I am mystified,' I said. 'I don't like to have my logic demolished. Where is the third man?'

We drove on along the long flat road to Seville, to Seville the old capital of the Spanish kings, where now a Captain-General holds the Army Command.

As we drove, dusk came slowly over Andalusia. So wide and empty are the horizons of Spain, that every night there is a sunset of strange beauty. That night it was all saffron glow, furled pink and grey scarves.

Once or twice I checked at a high wall, suspecting a cemetery. 'We are too far inland now,' said George. 'Drowned corpses here stick to the coast. Cease snuffling, ghoul. We are coming to the living beauties of Seville, to the Bodega below stairs.'

So the sunset yielded to night, and as the stars, so large in Spain, came out, we drove up the mile known as the Reina Maria Avenue, all palms and orange trees.

4
THE SEVILLE DANCERS

We arrived in Seville at five minutes after midnight, just too late, as George rightly said, for dinner, which at 11 p.m. would still have been served. There were, however, quantities of dry sack in the city, and, in the bodega cellar of the Hotel Cristina, small dishes of almonds and stuffed olives. Above all there was the dance.

Some Spanish dancers will tell you that the best school of dance is now in Madrid. I do not know, but if so, there is still no setting for the dance like Seville.

'You will see the flamenca girls,' said George, 'and one particularly if she is still here – also a couple who do an act of thought transmission. Kary Mayer and Mery Dugan. He flits about the tables and talks with the customers. She is blindfolded and tells us what he is saying and what he has in his hand. Maybe there is a code.'

'Thought transmission is the simplest explanation,' I suggested. 'A code would be too complicated.'

The musicians struck up, the castanets began to chatter, and the tall graceful dancers began to fill the vaults of the bodega with their flamenca and fandango dances. Now and then an intermittent voice chanted the cholas, a thin sad voice full of meaning, and then again there was a zapateado, the aristocratic ancestor of the American tap dance, with a rhythmic ecstasy of stamping feet, while the slender young men watched their own toes, laughed and tossed back their heads like colts, and neatly held the hem of their boleros as they danced. Quicker and livelier it grew, sometimes they faced us and sometimes the tapping of feet yielded to the click of fingers and of castanets and with a whirl of skirts and petticoats, they were into a seguidilla. The thin voice rose and guided them, chanting, so it seemed, across the bare distance of Spanish land.

These were not the dances of physical delight. They showed instead grace and spirit, striving yet measured; they showed the conflict of pride and passion, the eventual victory of the one over the other. There was neither the leering nor wriggling of the modern dance hall. The curls of the heads glistened; the girls' hands wove arabesques over their heads, as their bodies began to stir to the music and they flashed smiles and frowns at each other, and laughed and talked as the figures brought them together. The music stopped as suddenly as the starting clash, and the dancers stood poised and still, panting a little.

Mery Dugan, the reader of thoughts, was a slight dark-haired figure in a spangled white evening dress. Her sunburnt shoulders and violet eyes contrasted well with it. As she came to the microphone and was blindfolded, she relaxed and was no more a woman, but seemed a little child in a party frock, reciting as she was told to do. Rapidly Kary Mayer shot his questions at her.

'This man has a letter in his hand. Where does it come from? What is the postmark?'

At first her answers were as swift as the question. As the

questions continued and Kary insisted on more and more detail, her answers came more slowly. They were consistently right. She showed signs of mental fatigue.

'What am I holding?'

'A bank note.'

'What is it?'

'A pound note.'

'Be more explicit.'

'A Gibraltar pound note.'

'What is its number?'

Mery Dugan quoted the serial numbers. George, who had held the pound note furtively behind the table was impressed.

'Maybe these two would help you in your search for the body,' he said, and, when the act was over, Kary and Mery joined us for a drink, watching the dancers, whose excitement rose in short cries as they set and wove. We asked Kary to tell us the story of his thought act, and this he related to us, the story of Kary and Mery.

Kary first discovered Mery as a child in Buenos Aires, afflicted by somnambulism. He set about trying to control her and cure her, then to studying for that purpose books on hypnotism and medicine. His study and treatment of her took eleven years and it passed from controlling her while she was sleep-walking to suggesting thoughts to her while she was conscious. In time he was able to pass his thoughts to her. Her act was that of a child still, like Du Maurier's Trilby.

We noticed something phonetic in their contact; for she had mistaken the postmark of a letter from Algiers for Algeciras. Of signs there could be no question, as she was blindfolded, and his voice was not greatly modulated as he rapped out his questions to her. I could see no physical explanation for it. His cheek muscles flexed a little as he worked. Ventriloquism? – I hardly think so.

'My friend here is looking for a body,' said George. 'A grave without a name, or rather with a false name on it. Even that false name he does not know.'

'That is certainly a difficult search,' said Kary Mayer.

The music rose and fell, the thin voice of the wizened tenor took command of the dancers again. Mery Dugan sat back dreamily, nodding, I fancied, at a conversation that she need not lean forward to follow.

'My friend is an optimist,' said George.

'Optimism is fey,' said Kary Mayer. 'Perhaps he will find this grave.'

'Could you help us to find it?' I ventured, and Kary thought hard and long.

'Imagine a body ten years ago floating in to the coast of Spain. To its wrist is attached a pouch containing important papers. The papers are false, the body is real, but its name is false. It is buried near the coast, but we do not know where. Where is it?'

'I will concentrate this night on your problem for an hour or so,' said Kary Meyer; and Mery Dugan, leaning back and listening either to the music or to his thoughts, nodded to herself. She was now a woman again, and the little girl in her had crept back within the recesses of the past.

'Perhaps Mery can help us,' said Kary Mayer. 'She is a powerful medium. But these are indeed few details that you have given us.'

'That is what my friend feels too,' said George, and we all laughed together.

'If you find the grave,' said Kary, 'and the inscription on it – you say it is false – maybe I can tell you who is really in it.'

The castanets clashed away at the bodega vaults, the morning hours drew on, Kary and Mery withdrew and we left the guitars still twanging and made our way up to bed, sleeping in a suite decorated with tempera murals of the chase.

'She wasn't there,' said George.

'Who wasn't?'

'The particular flamenca girl.'

'Are flamenca girls particular?'

Seville slept.

There was a hiatus at the Consulate-General. The post of H.M. Consul-General was vacant, until the Foreign Office should fill it from London; the Consul had gone to Gibraltar, and the Vice-Consul was on leave. A Pro-Consul, Mr Fussell, was driving up from Jerez, having been sent to fill the gap by our friend the Vice-Consul Guy Williams of Humbert and Williams.

Until Mr Fussell arrived there was nobody who had the combination to the casket in which the keys of the safe reposed, and in the safe lay the register of graves for the whole Seville area which was the object of our search. Fussell was still that morning driving up Hannibal's road, and we could do nothing but await his arrival. Waiting also for him was a merchant seaman from Seville docks with a grievance, and the next of kin of an aged British subject, Mr Bellamy, who had died in the night.

We picked and smelled a fragrant bitter orange from the trees outside the Consulate-General and walked along to the Giralda to climb the cathedral tower.

The tower is Moorish, built by Djabir, one of the architects of the Almohades. Nine feet thick in stone at the base, the walls thicken as you mount the thirty-five planes, and the stair consequently becomes narrower, until from its dark slope you emerge on the sunlit parapet of what was once the minaret of Seville. Below lay the lead and copper roof of what was decided in 1401 by the Dean and Chapter to be 'so great a cathedral to be built that posterity will say we were mad to attempt it'.

The tower has a Renaissance summit and statue of the patron saint, replacing a gigantic bar bearing four gilded copper apples, so large that a gate of Seville had to be widened to admit one of them. These apples were shaken down after a century or so by the earthquake of 1395.

Through the shining mists of the Guadalquivir we could see the cranes on the wharves where the cargoes are loaded for England, the wharves where Fritz Baumann's Spanish agents skulked to place their time-bombs. We could see below us into the courtyard of the Alcazar, the residence first of the Almohades Emirs, one of whom, Mo Tamid, had laid out a garden with the heads of his enemies from the rival Emirate of Cordoba. I wonder how long this garden delighted him. Another Emir of Seville bought a respite from the Christian conquerors by giving his daughter to Alfonso III in marriage, and so between 1069 and 1248 Seville remained in Moorish hands.

Pedro the Cruel lived in this Alcazar, and murdered there his own brother, the Master of Santiago. There too his mistress, Maria di Padilla, bathed in what had once been a Moorish bath, and the obedient gallants of Pedro's court sipped her bath water in homage, though one of them demurred on the pretext lest 'having tasted the sauce he might be suspected of coveting the partridge'.

The taller modern blocks of Seville lay between us and Italica, the settlement requisitioned by Scipio for some of his foot-weary veterans from Africa, who preferred the suburban life of Seville to the prospect of marching back all the way to Rome. There would be no doubt of my choice either.

We found time for a walk round the cathedral, with its double aisles and immense breadth. Here come the American tourists, flashing through Seville, to pass a minute or so at the monument where the ashes of Christopher Columbus are preserved. Here too come whispering beggars, with sad severe faces, to pluck at your sleeve.

Toledo, the steel town, may have won the struggle for primacy in Spain, but its cathedral cannot compare with this.

'I have come to enquire about a corpse,' I asked Pro-Consul Fussell on returning to the Consulate-General.

'He hasn't come up yet,' said Mr Fussell. 'He only went over the side last night, and he's still somewhere in the river. There was a note left in his cabin and a trail of blood across the deck to the ship's rail. You do mean the second mate of the *Pinto*, don't you?'

'No, I am looking for an officer who was drowned at sea ten years ago, and is buried somewhere in the Seville command.'

'What's his name?'

'I don't know.'

'Don't you know his regiment?'

'Neither.'

'Something then?'

'I can give you the date of his burial to within a month or so. There cannot be many on this coast. March, April, May or June 1943.'

'Well, let's look in the register.'

Pro-Consul Fussell opened the safe and began to peruse the papers.

'Will a deserter do? Private Gilbert, deserted from Gibraltar, died in Seville?'

'No use at all.'

The Pro-Consul ran through the register of graves – Cadiz, Jerez, Huelva, Palaciado de la Frontera.

'It's the coast that matters,' I said.

'There were two Beaufighter pilots lost in the Huelva area,' said Fussell. 'Might he have been R.A.F.?'

'Unlikely.'

'Can't you tell me more about him?'

So I sat down and told Fussell what I suspected to be true – how a man already dead, so Westphal's book showed, had been used as a decoy with false papers to deceive the enemy somewhere on this coast.

Then I related the perplexing story of the Catalina crashing in the sea in 1942, and the two dead bodies washed up, and the littered secret papers that had lain unclaimed in the Spanish tunny-canning factory at Barrosa. So much Mr Williams had confirmed, but he seemed not to know anything of a third man.

'If there was a third man,' said Fussell, 'would you not think that the body would hardly be posted to that part of the coast where the first accident happened?'

That seemed to make sense.

'Was your man a Church of England or R.C.?'

'How should I know?' I groaned.

'Well, if he was a Roman Catholic he would not be in this register. This covers English cemeteries only.'

This was the heaviest news that we had heard so far.

'What if he was Roman Catholic?'

'I couldn't help you there. You would have to consult the register in the Spanish graveyards.'

'Then we may well have passed him by between Gibraltar and here?'

'Perhaps you have. Perhaps he has been taken away altogether – buried at sea.'

'As I understood it, he had to be buried normally on the spot. Otherwise the deception might not have worked.'

I retraced my way to the Hotel Cristina. A hurdy-gurdy outside the hotel played the tune of the *Third Man*. I gave him a peseta.

'Could we ask the Archbishop of Seville?' I suggested to George.

'The Archbishop could hardly help us,' thought George. 'The Archbishop is a severe character who disapproves of modern dancing, films and bathing suits. Yet he sanctions each year the Dance of the Seises, a sort of minuet that ten choristers dance in costume with castanets before the high altar of the cathedral.'

'What about the Captain-General?'

'There is a new Captain-General in Seville. The Consuls are new, the chaplains are new. It all makes your search harder.'

We strolled down to the bodega again. The flamenca girls were rehearsing their dances. Four hours a day it takes them to keep an edge on their talent. Out of the changing rooms they swung carelessly, in various stages of dress, in working garb and practised languidly as the mood took them, calling to each other, laughing, pointing. It was as if we were not there.

'You are going to write a book,' said George, 'and then people will come and discover my bodega. They will crowd down these cellar stairs and stare and chew. Worse still, when the book is read a film theme will occur to Hollywood about flamenca girls. It will turn upon the U.S. bases to be set up here, and a G.I. with a well-known Hollywood face will come sloping in and sit down there, just where you are sitting, hunched forward, chewing olives. Suddenly the music will stop and Elvira, the most beautiful of all the flamenca girls, will stroll over to his table. He doesn't react the least bit. Everybody turns in their direction. She casts him one stormy look. Speaks one word. Now he's on his feet and they go into a clinch. The flamenca lads give up and melt away, because they cannot compete. He has something they haven't, you and I haven't got. That is what the written word can do to my bodega.'

'How can I write a book if my search doesn't succeed?'

George took me on to lunch with Senor Borbolla and his English wife in a cool, quiet house with wrought-ironwork doors in

47

the mezquita off the Plaza Santa Cruz, a square full of orange trees round a fountain.

'My friend was asking whether flamenca girls are particular,' ventured George at the fourth sherry. 'My theory is that there is so much hard work in mastering the dance that a flamenca girl cannot have anything of the private life of a Hollywood actress. She cannot languish on the set, go to cocktail parties, night clubs to the small hours, country clubs and millionaires' houses. She has to work hard to keep herself at the height of the art. The gestures, the movements of the dance are a renunciation even of what they express, voluptuousness and love. There is an academic chastity in these dances that makes them more piquant. They play with the receding likelihoods of love, and when the dances are over in the light of morning grey, an old duenna, who was once herself a flamenca girl, fetches them at the door and accompanies them home through the streets of Seville.'

Senor Borbolla had listened to this poetic theory from a visitor to Seville with the gravest of Spanish politeness. He leaned back, a man with a wealth of experience, and remarked:

'What you say in many words means perhaps in few that the flamenca girl has no steady chap.'

'That is it, just that.'

'Steady love,' said Don Borbolla, 'would be the death of the flamenca girl. Chastity? – her chastity is the independence of the artist. Of course there is love, persuasion, anger – a good slap in the face may be helpful at the critical moment. Do not try that at the wrong moment though. It might have terrible consequences for you.'

We ate spiced dishes and drank Rioja wine late into the Spanish afternoon, looking at the green leaves in his shaded patio.

'Ask the Germans in Seville,' suggested George, and so I enquired about them, and got the address of Count Leventzow in the Calle Luis Montoto.

The Count was a portly man of some height with a florid face and a jovial manner. His house lay in an avenue of plane trees with the appearance of a French boulevard. The rooms, large, white-washed, were hung with the stiff portraits of his North German and Danish ancestors. He poured out a beaker of sherry. The Leventzow furnishings all around us gave the atmosphere of a German castle – baroque commodes, an oak table, silver dishes!

'I did not have to return to Germany after the war,' said the Count simply; 'the Duke of Alba and the Infanta interceded for me. So I have been fortunately able to keep my possessions here.'

Then followed the usual explanation of which Germans unburden themselves – the extent to which the Count had collaborated with the Nazis in their decade of power. Business as usual had been the Count's formula – 'I served the State'. He had put up, he said, strenuous resistance to the encroachments or stupidities of the Party in his consular territory. Lordly objections through diplomatic channels to the unwanted activities in Spain of the National Socialist Organisation of Germans Abroad! Quite easy, no doubt, for Consul-General Count Leventzow, but no game evidently for humble Consul Schmidt to play! The Count had been Head of the Protocol in 1936, in Berlin, and had organised many a reception and approved many a table order in the Chancellery of the Führer.

He even recalled organising a special luncheon for Sir Robert Vansittart to meet Hitler in 1936, and claimed that it had been quite a harmonious occasion – said that they had understood each other's point of view.

What of the body?

'The dispatches of a British courier drowned on the Seville district coast? Of course I kept away from all intelligence work. I was most careful,' said the Count, 'but I would have certainly heard something if our people in Seville had managed to see those papers.

No, the dispatches will probably have been sent on unopened to Madrid.'

Heavily the Count lumbered out to see me into the car. It seemed that our search of Seville was at its end. George had received an impatient telephone call from the Rock Hotel. The P. and O. boat was in. He revved the engine, itching to go. Before driving out of Seville I picked, as an appropriate memory of the city, a bitter orange.

5

THE GRAVE IN HUELVA

Mile after mile the sports car laid back. Once we nearly hit a goat in the dusk, drooling across the road towards a thatched shanty. The sunset of Spain spread its vast canvas to a few solitary creatures and then night wiped it away. As the stars came out we ran into Jerez. The streets of Jerez were crowded with people, excited shouting people.

'It is a feast day,' said George. 'Fiesta.'

Three gorgeous kings, one sitting on a palanquin, two riding on horseback, passed slowly down the main street. Turbanned Moors escorted them. Franco's cavalry in fancy dress threw bonbons into the crowd.

'It is the feast of the three kings today,' said George. 'We won't make Gib tonight.'

In the main square of Jerez an army searchlight projected its beam onto the manger scene on a stage. Overhead a papier-mâché star crept slowly along a wire. We withdrew to the nearest bar and waited for the procession to disperse.

'I think all the Consuls have been telling you what they know,' said George. 'There must be some explanation. What about trying the Malaga coast?'

'The omens said Seville.'

'Try Don Williams again,' suggested George. 'He is a wise bird. He won't be at his bodega at this time of night.'

'Ask him what is the proper way of tracing an R.C.'

I rang up the patriarchal house, asked for Don Guido Williams, and Don Guido came to the phone.

Outside the band played loudly and the procession moved past.

'How would a Consulate keep trace of a British subject who died in the area if he was a Roman Catholic?' I asked. 'He would not be in our register of graves because that only covers the English cemeteries.'

Don Guido replied:

'There is a register of graves and a register of deaths. If a British subject is not in the one, he would be in the other. That has all denominations.'

'The register of deaths?'

'That is so,' said Don Guido.

Outside the crowds were thinning. No sooner was I in the car than George began to pick his way through.

'Any clue?'

'Don Guido says there is a second register, the register of deaths.'

A few miles further on, I said: 'I must go back – back to Seville.'

'Not tonight,' said George. 'We don't.'

He pressed on towards the coast, and an hour later we were passing the white, glistening salt heaps in the marshland behind Cadiz.

A little further on there is a section of the road that I am told is full of Roman pottery remains. The Spaniards have been excavating the road banks to widen it, and have cast up all sorts of bits and pieces. The headlights lit up a stretch where the road was under repair, and there we stopped and stumbled up the sandy bank into the wild olive shrubs. Everywhere we kicked up bits of pottery, coarse strong earthenware, bits of a form of jar common in these parts that has a pointed base.

'So you can stick it upright in the sand,' George suggested.

'So that nobody would want to steal it, I expect, like some London fire buckets that roll over if you put them on the ground. These would only be useful if you have one of those wrought-iron cradles to stand them in.'

There wasn't a single pitcher in one piece. Not half a jar! The pieces were fragmentary.

'Export rejects,' grunted George and picked his way back to the car. We arrived weary at Algeciras in the early hours, stayed at the Cristina Hotel, and were back in Gibraltar next day. I could see then why George had hurried back. From now on evidently I must continue the search alone.

The bar of the Rock was fuller at midday than I had expected, and so I found a certain interest as I spread my road map and marked off the areas already searched. There were perplexing gaps. I felt that I might have to reconnoitre San Lucar and Bonanza and then Huelva.

'But you cannot get from San Lucar to Huelva,' they explained, 'because of the Marisma, the marsh behind the Arenas Gordas coast.'

'What about a steamer?'

'There is no steamer. You must go by road and via Seville.'

'All that way inland?'

Well, I would go by Seville then, and see if there was a register of deaths. But would the Consul allow his register of deaths to be perused? Was that not perhaps a more confidential document even than a mere register of graves?

Huelva, which at first had seemed remote to me, seemed to gain in importance as I studied the map. For on either side of it stretched miles of desolate coast. It would evidently be the resting place for all drowned corpses from a wide area. Beyond it was Isla Cristina, and then the Guadiana River and Portugal. That would indeed be the end.

There is something more profoundly interesting in travelling poor than in travelling rich, since time cannot matter any more. You carry your own baggage. You eye cars for lifts. You sit and wait for 'buses. You meet and talk to strange characters. That is the proper pace and mood in which to search for a grave. Don Pedro, the taximan who drives you to Gibraltar ferry quay gates, told me that he had often gone all over Spain with his taxi, taking tourists about.

'But the distances are too much in the end, and now I will only drive them round in this area. Seville, Malaga, no further!'

'I think you are mad to go back,' said George, as I waved good-bye to them outside the Rock Hotel. 'You can't find him. I don't believe there ever was such a person.'

Now I had no friendly car to charge from cemetery to cemetery, and less pesetas than I should have liked. It was Epiphany Tuesday. Don Pedro explained my route to me. There is lively sympathy for anybody in Spain who is travelling the hard way. Take the ferry, he advised, to Algeciras, the 'bus onwards through Medina Sidonia. At the quay the dockyard workers from Algeciras, some of them the men who in wartime had done small intelligence jobs for Fritz Baumann, were slouching on board the ferry, their pockets bulging with contraband packets of tobacco from the tobacco factory. On deck, as we pulled away from the quayside in the dusk, black-clad old wives seemed to be crossing themselves, muttering as they did so. In reality they were not praying; they were sliding tobacco packets

into the folds and linings of their blouses and skirts. With gestic-
ulations and incantations, with shrilling of laughter, the whole
second-class deck went through this vesper routine as the ferry
steamed across the bay to the lights westward. At Algeciras harbour
gates there was a large hamper set, and into that hamper the Spanish
docks police threw at least one packet from the person of each trav-
eller. The packet was usually neatly displayed at breast-pocket level
with one corner sticking out and ready to be surrendered. The police
took their perquisites. The rest went in free.

I was seized by a ragged Moor who took my bag. Children ran
alongside us. I found there was no 'bus till the next day. Once more
it was the Hotel Cristina; and since it happened to be a fiesta, once
more there was a ball in preparation. Dancers had come from Seville,
Elvira Eory, Pacatores and Maria Martin, and the impersonator and
compère Tommy Castels. There was also a conjurer who ate glass,
and an 'alto with a black fringe in the mode of Toulouse-Lautrec.
Among those who sat ordering champagne round the floor was a
curly-headed man with bulbous eyes who took in the whole cabaret with an authoritative stare (this was the Mayor of Algeciras), a
friendly Irishman from Dublin, the manager Lieb and his wife and
a number of English tourists.

Evidently some great anguish was tugging at the heart of the
master of ceremonies Tommy Castels. His act was eccentric. He
clowned. He plagued the singer, he interrupted the dancers. Yet
it was his imitation of an Italian tenor that was the highlight of
the evening. At one moment it seemed that an argument might
be involving both him and the Mayor, but the glass-eating conjurer intervened and the thundercloud passed over. Next morning,
Tommy Castels and I climbed into the 'bus together for Seville.

Tommy was a talkative and friendly companion. The 'bus took
a hilly road away from the coastal plains. Now and then it stopped

at a tavern and out climbed the whole coachload to drink red wine (tinto) at the bar and eat sliced squid and broiled lamb. The difficulty was to spend any pesetas, for Tommy the compère would pay for everything.

'A visitor to Spain cannot pay,' he said simply. A Moroccan from Tangier in a tartan shirt who claimed to be an intimate friend of the British Consul said exactly the same thing. That was positively so.

'If we should visit England and travel in your 'buses,' they said, 'you will wish to pay at the halts. That is another matter entirely.'

Eventually we came to the square white casas of Medina Sidonia, crowding up the slopes of a steep hill. The beggars and the idiots drew round like flies, plucking at our sleeves with morose, severe looks. Tommy brushed them off and called for 'Tinto!' He began to run through his act at the bar, imitated a brace of partridges calling, a dog flushing them both, a right and left; a crying baby, a muleteer arguing with his mule, a laying hen, a pig at rest.

We stopped many times setting down and taking up passengers. Invariably Tommy the clown ordered 'Tinto!' It was dark when we got to Seville, and Tommy found quarters in the most extraordinary hotel that I have yet seen, the Hotel de Madrid, a big rambling palace in the Hispano-Moresque style, all black marble and white stucco arabesque friezes, with glass-enclosed patios, flagged passages and a quantity of furnished landings and galleries. It had once been the residence of the Dukes of Gelves, who had evidently not built it with the idea of converting it later into an hotel.

Next morning there was an early 'bus to Huelva. If I took that, it would be too late on my return to go to the Consulate-General in Seville again the same day. If I went to the Consulate-General, I would miss the 'bus to Huelva. The Consul might not be back from Gibraltar. He would perhaps find it inadvisable to show me the register.

I pondered on the advisability of ringing up the Vice-Consul in Huelva and asking him. But this was a new Vice-Consul, Mr Robert Sinclair, and he would be unlikely to have any first-hand knowledge of what happened in 1943. Nor would he be at the Vice-Consulate so early in the morning. Besides, being as all Vice-Consuls, an acting and honorary personage, he was known to divide his time between that office and the Tharsis Tobacco Company. So much I had learned in Gibraltar, so I decided that Huelva too must be visited personally. If nothing was to be found there, I could pester the Seville Consulate-General on my return journey the following day to show me the register of deaths for the whole area. So it was the 'bus for Huelva, over the Guadalquivir, where perhaps the body of the second mate of the *Pinto* still lay bedded, up the hill of Niebla with its castle wall, and on towards the valley of the Rio Tinto, which flows discoloured with the effluence of the mines, through the Marisma down to the port of Columbus – and into the Gulf of Cadiz, the many-hued Rio Tinto.

Huelva is described as having an excellent winter climate. That is all that there is to recommend it; its main roads are those of a busy port, its buildings of little interest. I walked through depressing streets, dusty, brightly sunlit, full of barefoot children, to the place where its cemetery was marked on my ancient Baedeker. I found there empty walls – waste land – there was not a grave left.

Mr Robert Sinclair, the Vice-Consul, told me when I called on him at the Calle 18 Julio, that the cemetery, both cemeteries, had indeed been moved outside Huelva.

Yes, he had a register of deaths as well as a register of graves. What name was I looking for? If I could tell him the name, he would see if he could confirm it.

This was just the same response as other Vice-Consuls and Pro-Consuls had given me on my search through Spain. It was eminently reasonable. I had visited cemeteries before, plied the cemetery keepers with questions and come away fairly satisfied. I must obviously go on searching the hard way. But where was the cemetery?

'It has all been moved to a place three miles outside the town,' said the Vice-Consul. 'You will have to walk or take a taxi. I should take a taxi.'

Martinez the taximan, who had already overcharged me once for a ride to the Vice-Consul's office, was grinning as I came out. One hundred pesetas was his price to the cemetery. I thought bitterly of George, now miles away on the Malaga coast, and climbed in. The taxi creaked and groaned down a dusty lane between cactus hedges through the arid countryside. At last there was a high white wall ahead. I had come to know these high white walls, set with the niche graves where Spaniards bury their dead above ground.

Outside the cemetery, a few beggars and boys gathered round the taxi. This was indeed an unusual place for a taxi to be. I asked for the cemetery keeper. They explained that he was away in Huelva. There was only a gravedigger there. So I must look for myself, and first I visited thoroughly the little English cemetery. There indeed were the two Beaufighter men whose aircraft had crashed inland, lying under clean white stone crosses; there was an English lad whose name I knew, some Victorian headstones, a Spaniard or two, and that was all. I turned to the gates of the main cemetery.

At this sight my heart sank. Of the many cemeteries I had seen on this coast, Tarifa, Jerez, Gibraltar, Chiclana, Veher, this was indeed the largest. I do not know how Huelva cemetery compares in size with Cadiz, which had been obligingly searched for me, but Huelva's antiquity is as great as that of Cadiz, perhaps even greater. It is variously said to have been a Phoenician and a Roman settlement, identified by some with a legendary Tharsis and by others with Onuba. Certainly a large congregation had been moved when the fathers of Huelva decided to transfer their cemetery outside the town. Martinez consulted the gravedigger, and the gravedigger suggested that the Englishman might care to see the register. This gravedigger was a practical man.

I discovered that the register was kept in a fair clerical hand, and that it was in chronological order. How much time this discovery might have saved us earlier in the search! I began to turn the pages from February 1943 onwards, and saw suddenly the familiar word 'Cardiff'. This was grave number 3913 in walk 0469, and the name was W. Martin, a married man (Casado) whose age was between 35 and 40. *Asfyxia* – that meant that he had been drowned. A likely find!

There was by now a congregation of urchins, eager and anticipating pesetas if they found the grave. Rapidly they spread out across the churchyard, some looking at the tombs, and some the wall niches. The gravedigger moved more slowly through this 'town without a market', until a faint shout from one place brought us to a flat granite slab.

Julio Diaz, a friend of the taxi driver, had found him. The slab was marked with a simple inscription:

WILLIAM MARTIN

BORN 29TH MARCH 1907

DIED 24TH APRIL

1943

BELOVED SON OF JOHN GLYNDWYR MARTIN

AND THE LATE ANTONIA MARTIN OF CARDIFF, WALES.

So far I was disappointed, and read the inscription with a sinking feeling. Then the last line revived my hopes.

DULCE ET DECORUM EST PRO PATRIA MORI.

Major Martin's grave in Huelva

How did he die for his country, then, at this remote place, so far from any battlefield? The dates were probable, if my theory held. Only the rank of an officer was missing from the headstone. I paused for a moment and noted it all down.

Still dubious, I was led round other graves, shown that of Georges Forestier, the French aviator who crashed his aircraft here on 4 September 1911, the graves of two famous bullfighters, and then, with a shower of pesetas to the search party, the taxi lurched off to Huelva again.

'Did you find your war grave?' asked the Vice-Consul, whom I met again just outside the Vice-Consular office.

'I think I have found the man in the Spanish cemetery. Would you have any record of a W. Martin, died April 24th, 1943?'

'Come inside,' said Mr Sinclair, and he turned up the register of deaths in the cramped little office.

'Yes, there is a W. Martin, drowned, buried on May 2nd, 1943.'

'Are there no more particulars than that?'

'He is described as a Major, Royal Marines.'

I went to Baez photographic studio in one of the Arcades of Huelva, and found there an enterprising photographer. Once more the grinning Martinez steered us down the cactus-hedged lane. Once more the urchins gathered at the grave as we photographed it. None knew who really lay beneath, and only I suspected the grim hoax behind it all. As for W. Martin, whoever he was, it would hardly have occurred to him what a turmoil his identity and whereabouts would cause after death.

There was little more to be done in Huelva. I read the name of the stonemason, M. Toscano, and the resourceful Julio told me that his yard was in Zafra Street. We set out for Zafra Street and learned from the mason that Don Martin's stone had been ordered by a British Vice-Consul many years ago. He gave us the name of Haselden, and that was all.

Who was this Martin? In the 'bus back to Seville, I pondered on the case. This must be the man – the date of his burial just two months before the landings in Sicily took place – time enough for the false information that he carried to filter through to Berlin, for all manner of cross checks to be made on his identity. Was this really he? The enigmatic quotation on his grave would seem to suggest it. Perhaps there would be something more about him to be learned when I reached Madrid.

There was hardly any need in Seville now to call on Consul Draeger or Consul Wolff, the two ex-German officials whose wartime memory might have helped me. For the sake of form, I visited the British Consul's office and found him back from Gibraltar and preparing to move to Berlin. There seemed to be little static about Her Majesty's Consulate-General in Seville. We talked of living conditions in Berlin. I enquired whether the second mate of the *Pinto* had been found. The Consul seemed to be surprised that I did not wish to borrow money, ask him to bury a body, register a birth, or pay my passage home. It was with evident relief that he saw me go.

Kary Mayer and Mery Dugan were at their act in the bodega of the Cristina Hotel. She stood there, like a little child at the microphone, repeating what was in his mind.

Afterwards I spoke to them, told them of my search, of the grave and the name on the grave. Who was he really? I put the question to Kary and he thought long about it, but this was a test beyond perhaps even the powers of a medium. Major Martin had no craving to reveal himself, and I have not since heard from Kary and Mery that they have discovered his identity.

In the bodega, the flamenca girls danced, the guitarist picked thoughtfully at his chords, the young men cried 'Olé'. The German Count sat doubtless alone among his Baltic furnishings, drinking to his ancestors and congratulating himself on the firmness that he had once displayed towards the encroachments of the Nazis on the private lives of Germans in the Seville area. I crept back to the Hotel de Madrid through the empty streets of Seville. Tommy Castels, the compère, had invited me to see his show, and much as I would have enjoyed a little comedy I felt the need of sleep. In the vast antique palace of the Duke of Gelves, the thought of the grave made me a little uneasy. It isn't healthy to speculate too much about the dead, but there was no apparition that night. Whoever he was, the man in Huelva slept soundly.

6

THE QUEST IN LONDON

I had still no positive proof that I had found the drowned courier who had figured so much already in both fiction and military memoirs. There was so far no more than strong suspicion.

Back in Madrid Captain Wilhelm Lenz came eagerly to a café in the Calle Antonio to hear what I had to say. By then the photograph of Don Martin's grave had reached me and I passed it over to him. He stared at it and read the inscription.

'I am able to tell you something more,' he said.

Since you say that it was in Huelva that the body was washed up, it may have been my agent in Huelva who notified me of it and not the man in Cadiz. I cannot be sure so many long years afterwards.

But I do recollect what it was that I was shown here in Madrid. It was two folded letters that had been evidently taken from the courier's pouch. I think that they were signed by a high officer in London.

One was on War Office notepaper. I think that these letters were addressed to General Alexander, and they advised him of the strategy which he must consider for the next amphibious campaign.

I recollect that these letters mentioned the operational name 'Husky'. That stuck in my memory, because it seemed to me a dangerous thing to name the codeword in the same document as discussed the possible destinations.

If I suggested to you in my last talk – I cannot quite remember – that it was photostats of these letters that my Spanish agent in the General Staff showed me, I must correct that impression. It was actually the original letters that I saw and held in my hands for about an hour. During that time I took them to the basement of the German Embassy and had my photographer photo-copy them there. I even stood over him while he worked, so that he could not read the documents. They seemed to me to be of the highest importance.

This impression was fortified when I heard that Sir Samuel Hoare, the British Ambassador, had made urgent demands with the Ministry of Foreign Affairs to recover the despatch case that the courier had been carrying.

You will want me to try and recall the contents of these letters. As far as I can recollect they spoke of the future strategy of the Allies in the Mediterranean in the spring of 1943. They mentioned as possible targets for landings Greece and the Dodecanese, as well, I think, as Corsica or Sardinia, but did not suggest Sicily. However, the final choice seemed to be left to the General to whom they were addressed, General Alexander.

I sent the photostats off to Berlin by the hand of the assistant air attaché, Captain Philipp von Kühlenthal, son of the General. So you can see that I attached some importance to them at the time. As I say, I found the strategic considerations not definite enough to suggest an already fixed target on the north Mediterranean coast. So I don't see that I was misled. Yet I have read a short report in a German newspaper which suggests that there was some such hoax.

'I believe that there was, and that this was the grave.' I tapped the photograph.

Old Lenz read aloud the inscription:

'Dulce et decorum est pro patria mori.'

It was beginning to dawn on him. He admitted the possibility with a long-drawn '*Schön!* Ach, if that is really so, I must congratulate them.' So ten years afterwards, Captain Lenz was beginning to straighten out the puzzle.

But memory without documents is deceptive, and so he wrote to the former German Vice-Consul in Huelva, an old man now purblind, whose son replied that nothing of a British courier's body being washed up had been known at the time or since either to his father or to anyone in the German colony of Huelva. It must have seemed a normal occurrence at the time.

The burly Baumann was a less quiescent and impressive visitor.

'Well,' asked the frogman, 'did you find the officer's body?'

I showed him the photograph of the grave, and said:

'I think that this courier was in fact the same man as the memoirs of General Westphal mention. He was not in fact drowned, but floated in as a decoy with false documents to deceive you people on our strategy in the Mediterranean theatre of war.'

This to Major Dr Fritz Baumann, the pathologist, was a blow from which he took a long time to recover.

'You mean that this body was not drowned, that the papers were faked.' He stared at me fixedly.

'So I believe.'

His eyes lit up, his face clouded as he realised that he had missed the chance of a pathologist's lifetime.

'At the time, I may have been at Algeciras, or Seville! How did this man die? How did he look when he was washed up? Was he supported by a lifejacket, or did he float up to the surface? What marks of injury did the body bear? What was the state of decomposition? How long had he been in the water?'

Fritz was possessed with the scientific demon.

'If he was held up by the lifejacket, then how did he drown? Was there aircraft wreckage? In flying accidents the faces are often crushed sideways. Was this the case? Who has seen this body?'

Then he remembered that all this had happened ten years ago, that the body had lain ten years in the earth, that the whole war which had made it seem so important to have an autopsy on Major Martin, had joined the immemorial past.

'I don't know if he had a Mae West, or what he looked like. Pretty high perhaps! But what would you have done if you had suspected a "plant" at the time?'

'My team would have been over the cemetery wall,' said the resolute Fritz. 'We would have opened the grave by night and flown your Major Martin to Berlin for an autopsy by Professor Mueller-Hess, our famous pathologist.'

Fritz Baumann lapsed into silence, brooding on the mischance that had stood between him and the weirdest autopsy of all time. Surely fate had been unkind to him! What would Hitler have said, when he read such an autopsy by Professor Mueller-Hess? What would Mueller-Hess have discovered?

But I had still to establish the facts of the case myself. It was no more than a strong probability that this was indeed the man. If I could find the former Vice-Consul who had ordered the gravestone in Huelva, then I would perhaps come a little closer to the truth.

It was Baumann who suggested to me – 'Ask Don Peters who worked for you British during the war.' And he described to me a man who had once been his enemy.

Don Alvarez Peters, otherwise Commander Alvarez Peters, was one of those undefinable characters who became an honorary attaché during wartime and served England with an intensity and a thoroughness that no mere Anglo-Saxon could attain. While the war was on, the indefatigable Don Alvarez had been padding about Madrid, driving up to San Sebastian, flitting over to Barcelona, hovering about Gibraltar, and smuggling British airmen out of Vichy France. Don Alvarez was a Spaniard to Spaniards and an Englishman to the English, but an Englishman who saw what he wanted and would not let red tape defeat him. Golf and the long week-end, tea parties here and cocktails there. What was all that to Don Alvarez? He had an intelligence mind, the senses of a beagle, and he was always breasting the scent and worrying his subject until he had exhausted it. And when he had killed it from exhaustion, sometimes he would return and sniff it over. It was once more Rudolf in Madrid who gave me a clue as to where to find Don Alvarez.

If he isn't at his villa near Seville, and if he isn't visiting in Lisbon, Don Alvarez will be staying at his flat in Madrid. Don Alvarez, said Rudolf, who did not know the famous Don Alvarez?!

Alvarez Peters was in Madrid and would see me. He had heard that I had written a book about the German intelligence chief, Admiral Canaris.

'I have always been interested in Canaris,' said Don Alvarez, settling down for a talk,

> because I had a feeling – it was no more than a feeling, mind you –
> that under certain circumstances, he might have been on our side.
> Does this bore you? Are you sure?

Now take for instance the lists of our Allied airmen interned at the frontier as they arrived from Europe. Canaris might have asked General Vigon, his friend the Air Minister, for lists of their names. Pretty queer names some of those fellows had too for R.A.F. pilots. But the Admiral never did. The traffic went on. Does this bore you? Do say if it bores you! The Admiral never did.

You may ask whether Canaris had those lists already from someone else. I do not think so.

Commander Alvarez paused for breath.

'If we had encouraged people like him – what am I saying – if we had not actively *dis*couraged them, the world might present a different picture today. But they always know better in London. They send people out here to tell me, to tell me about Spain. I who have forgotten about Spain more than they ever knew. Or they want me to go to London, to tell me about Spain there.'

This was a familiar pattern.

Commander Peters groaned and shook his head with some exasperation.

'You mean,' I said, 'that we should have sent some living body to have a yarn with Admiral Canaris and his people, instead of sending a corpse.'

'A corpse?'

'Yes, I am thinking of corpses today, because I have just come up from Huelva where I was visiting the grave of a man in my regiment, Major William Martin, Royal Marines.'

'Oh my God!' said Don Alvarez, jumping to his feet.

'The truth will be coming out now in fact,' I said.

'Kesselring's Chief of Staff – General Westphal – has mentioned it in his book on the German Army.'

'I do not know about Westphal's book,' said Don Alvarez guardedly. 'I have never read it.'

'Do you know about Major Martin?'

'I am sorry,' said Commander Peters, 'but I am not free to discuss some subjects. It is a matter of conscience.'

'I respect your conscience, Commander Peters. I expect that I shall hear more when I get to London.'

There was much to be learned from the silence of Don Alvarez Peters.

One last visit I had to make before leaving Madrid, and that was in a supreme attempt to find out what the Spanish government might know about Major Martin. I sought an interview with General Vigon, the Chief of Spanish General Staff. After waiting at G.H.Q. for some minutes in a conference room with a large portrait of Franco in a fur-lined greatcoat flung back to reveal his grey military tunic, I was shown into the office of the Chief of Spanish General Staff.

General Vigon is a dry, frail old man with a bright eye and a quiet selective turn of speech. His mind ranges on essential matters only, though he must in days gone by have studied similar escapades of intelligence to those I sought to describe to him. As I gradually brought the story of Major Martin to the point and mentioned false documents, General Vigon's eyes twinkled.

'Yes, yes,' he said, 'false papers. I understand they often do that.'

From the commanding height of the Chief of Staff, he could spare a wintry, mischievous smile at the thought of the hush-boys assiduously planting their documents on the enemy. It was an old ruse with which Spain as a neutral power was not unacquainted.

'I was Minister of Air at the time you describe,' he commented. 'I do not suppose that any documents have been kept on this case. Of the incident I myself know nothing.'

So there was nothing for it but to return to London, and see what the Service Ministries might have to say.

I caught the Santiago de Chile air liner at Madrid airport, and oddly enough found myself sitting next to a Queen's Messenger. This elderly and forbidding personage slept a little among his diplomatic bags and pouches, left them for a moment to go aft to that cabin where even Queen's Messengers go alone. I eyed his pouches speculatively. In such a moment in wartime, Fritz Baumann, who often travelled in the same civil aircraft as British couriers, would have deftly substituted an identical brief-case. The Queen's Messenger glared at me as he came back, since I was evidently showing too much interest in his baggage.

In London I made a visit to Somerset House and at once examined the register of births and deaths. There were many Martins, but not one whose birth in March 1907 coincided with a death in April 1943. Then there could be no such man. After a check on the Services casualties, which took another day, I came to that conclusion.

At the Royal Marine Office in Queen Anne's buildings, the marine orderly in blues showed me into the clerk's office.

'Captain Colvin, foreign languages, I remember you,' said the clerk.

That was not bad indeed for a memory of a temporary officer discharged eight years previously. A remarkable corps, the Royal Marines!

I wondered if he would remember anything about a temporary officer called Major William Martin, but I was not left long in doubt. The Colonel in the Military Secretary's office looked at me very oddly as I asked:

'I have come to make a rather intimate enquiry about a fellow-officer, Major William Martin, Royal Marines, who was buried in 1943 in Spain.'

'Major William Martin. Do I know about him? They only brought his papers in these last few days.'

'Then the Royal Marine Office had nothing about him at the time?'

'I don't suppose a thing.'

I went to the Admiralty and enquired there, but found that far from being forthcoming with details about this extraordinary case, the lips of the Admiralty were pretty heavily sealed. And the reason was not far to seek.

The operation with Major William Martin had been the work partly of the Royal Navy and partly of an organisation known as Special Operations Executive. The disruptive work of this organisation during the war will be remembered by many, not least by our Allies themselves.

For some time past, it had become plain to the survivors of that Service, most of them officers who had held wartime jobs in London, that certain secret operations could not remain secret for ever. Enemy memoirs would reveal bits and pieces of them, and there would be questions about them in the House of Commons. There had been revelations already. A whole series of gallant and ill-founded operations against the Germans in Holland had been discovered and exploited by the German Counter-Espionage with disastrous effect. Some scores of Allied agents and friendly civilians had been wiped out by the Gestapo after tricking the London authorities into sending more agents into the traps that had already caught so many. These were the disclosures already made in the memoirs of Lieutenant-Colonel Giskes,[1] the German Counter-Espionage Chief for Holland, Belgium and Northern France. But corroboration or denial of these facts, even the investigation by

1 *London Calling North Pole*, by H. J. Giskes. Published by William Kimber, London, 1953.

Inter-Allied Commission of Enquiry, of the possibilities of gross carelessness or treason had in such instances been frustrated by an order to burn the documentary records of Special Operations Executive after the war. The first inconclusive enquiries by Dutch and Belgian General Staffs into the continual disappearance of their agents had been foiled by the lack of the evidence contained in the German documents. When the German documents had been captured and the enquiries could have been usefully reopened with all available evidence, the destruction of the British documents – probably on security grounds – had already taken place. Such was the curious story that I had been told about certain Secret Service documents.

What if the same were to be the case with Major Martin? What if this pseudonymic character had been utterly wiped out of the records? Who could complete my story for me?

Happily this was not the case. By great good fortune, the absorbing interest that attached to these papers of Major Martin had been fully appreciated by others, besides whom my knowledge of the man was slight indeed.

The papers, which had changed hands once or twice, were still available, I was told, though not available to me – at that moment.

At the time that I had visited the British Embassy in Madrid, I had disclosed, conforming with an old journalistic ritual, something of the purpose of my visit to Spain to our diplomats there. A cipher cable to London had caused a stir in Whitehall; for oddly enough it had been decided not long before to release just these papers of Major Martin for publication. Nettled perhaps by the assertions of Lieutenant-Colonel Giskes that he had led the Secret Service around by the nose in Holland, Belgium and Northern France, embarrassed by the revelations of Herr L. C. Moyzisch that his agent Cicero had pried into the Most Secret papers of the British

Ambassador in Turkey, the authorities may have decided to display in turn that we also know a thing or two, that beneath the soft and indifferent exterior of the public school type, there lurks an opponent of skill and thoroughness, able to match himself with the best in the intelligence field.

Such may well have been the considerations that led to the release of the fascinating documents about Major William Martin. Two officials of the Ministry of Defence admitted that records of the case did exist. (Did I observe them on the official's desk, tucked away just out of reach?) I could not be permitted access to them, however, because it had been decided to give priority for the purpose of publication to an officer of the R.N.V.R. who had during the war had a great deal to do with the last voyage of Major Martin. After that there was a probability that I too might examine the documents.

It might now be at last possible to find out whether Captain William Maryngton of Duff Cooper's novel, and Major William Martin – how oddly alike the two names sounded – were in fact the same man, the same wistful failure in life who had found fulfilment in such a strange way after death. At last my search had turned up the documents!

7

A SHORT HISTORY OF PLANT LIFE

To understand the origins of Major William Martin's mission, you must go back to the origins of deception. Without some such excursion into the plant world, it would not be possible to grasp how this macabre idea of making a corpse tell lies came to birth. That ruse would only be thought up after a hundred others had been tried in simpler forms, some succeeding and some failing. And how far back need we go to discover a time when governments at war did not try to mislead each other – at war and in peacetime too? In remote antiquity they revelled in it – in more recent times Emperor Charles V remarked when he heard of a complaint from the King of England that the Emperor had twice lied to him at a meeting:

'He lies,' said the Emperor indignantly, 'I lied to him three times.'

Tyrants sent messages that lied and gifts that lied.

But by the end of the nineteenth century, deception was already such a nationalised industry that the practice had been settled in departments of the General Staffs. It was no longer the prerogative of the monarch. For proof we need only go to the records of the Dreyfus Affair to discover how deep-rooted deception was in officialdom even in the staid 1890s.

It was well known to European governments of the nineteenth century that traitors and unfriendly agents were after military secrets. The best way to render them innocuous was not to arrest them, but to supply them with false information. This technique became known to the French as '*intoxication*', to the Germans as '*Irreführung*', to the British as 'deception of the enemy'.

'Colonel Sandherr' (one of the German intelligence officers mentioned in the Dreyfus Affair) employed double agents – that is, agents who pretended to be German traitors and were actually instructed to transmit false information to military attachés. These agents communicated to the Statistical Section (of the German General Staff) those questions that they had received from the military attachés, and the Statistical Section furnished them with replies, half correct, half incorrect, or dilatory, but so phrased by the competent branch of the General Staff that no information prejudicial to national defence would reach the enemy.

Such was the evidence of Colonel Larpent about the Germans in the trial of Captain Dreyfus.

That the French had a similar technique as well, the evidence of Colonel Cordier at the Rennes Trial (Vol. I of the Précis of the Dreyfus Affair) shows us clearly enough. He speaks of exhibits – or false documents specially forged to mislead foreign powers.

'These documents were kept and classified with the greatest of care. The officers themselves had to do the classification and you may imagine with what particular care that was done. If you can imagine the enormous quantity of false information we were passing to the further side of the frontier, it was necessary not to make a single mistake. Every time a false piece of information was uttered, we had to be certain that it agreed with what had been said before.'

So it was that the two military powers of the Continent sought to outwit each other long before the First World War. This deception covered moments of weakness, it disguised concentrations of strength, it misled on strategy, on the time required for military movements and mobilisation, and on the performance of weapons. Every means of disseminating false information was tried in turn. Before attachés 'forgot' their 'most secret' papers in taxicabs, be sure that they forgot them in fiacres, in hansom cabs and in saddlebags. Be sure that they sometimes let a beautiful enemy agent have access to a safe or a strong box because the papers hidden in it were specially intended for the enemy. Be sure that they muttered indiscretions at the balls of the third Republic, and took large sums of money from the enemy intelligence officer for forged documents that it was their military duty to plant.

All this was well known to intelligence officers before the petrol engine was invented, before the British Official Secrets Act was passed. And this heady 'intoxication' brought after it disillusionment and scepticism – though there are new dupes born every minute and others who dupe themselves by firmly believing that their duperie is an entirely new invention.

By some higher law, the man who deals in plants becomes infected by the atmosphere of the planthouse. Indeed, it is possible in the memoirs of a secret agent to see him pull off one coup after another, until all unperceived to himself, his cleverness leads him into a false world. Whoever knows the whole picture can detect an error of fact. Sometimes, however, the whole picture has been so successfully distorted by a jungle of 'plants' that the essential truth appears itself to be an error. That is the object of the plant.

And who can really tell for what purpose he is interrogated? The Kaiser's agent, Dr Karl Armgaard Graves, found himself closely questioned by British intelligence officers after his arrest in 1912 about the information that the Kaiser might possess on the warships of the Royal Navy. Graves asserted with emphasis that the blueprints of certain capital ships of the Royal Navy had been betrayed to the German government. Was that so? Were not perhaps the British seeking to confirm through this captured agent that their 'plants' were being accepted as genuine by the Imperial German Navy? We can hardly discern the truth.

Yet one thing is certainly true of intelligence – the more that is known of counterfeit and counter-espionage, the more an officer is tempted to sit at his desk and speculate on the possibilities of deceit. In the end scepticism can triumph entirely. The real documents are on his desk. He doubts them. He doubts them because it seems more clever to be sceptical than to be credulous.

Have the dead ever served to deceive the enemy before? Was Major Martin the first to play this role? There may have been similar incidents in the First World War. Visualise an officer crawling forward in the dark into no-man's land to put deceptive papers in the tunic pockets of dead men. Visualise the enemy crawling out to go through those tunic pockets. Take deception a stage further. What of officers and men being served out with misleading material before they advanced into battle? Regulations were strictly against carrying papers, but there might be cases of 'carelessness'. Such ruses may well have been practised, studied and taught in intelligence courses between the two wars. They may even have been forgotten and conceived again.

I recall a portly major, stationed in Germany today, whose embonpoint and gaudy personality served throughout the war as a decoy to enemy agents in a neutral country. He was always to be seen, always to be met, always on his guard, and yet never doing anything. He was target number one for puzzled German and Italian counter-espionage. He was a living, walking, eating and drinking plant. He had flourish, he had panache. He must be a spy! All the time, a seedier and less flamboyant Briton was doing the real work. Of course, in a sense, that Major 'worked' too.

I met the Major in Germany after the war, and he told me of another ruse that foreran Major William Martin's mission by one generation. It was during the 1917 campaign when Allenby was pushing up the Palestine coast against the Germans and their Turkish allies.[2]

Yet knowledge that such plants had been successful in the past could in itself be a positive handicap in assessing a new situation. The men who had studied plants could not always see the real thing. Turn the clock on to 1940, and study the situation of the western allies during the 'phoney' war. There was no indication – only a powerful supposition – that Hitler would decide to attack through Holland and Belgium. He might break through via Switzerland into central France. He might even envelop the Maginot line in smoke and try and roll his whole panzer force across it. The French High Command was informed by its Service de Renseignements, so General L. Rivet, its former intelligence chief, told me ten years later, *'vous pouvez être attaqué à chaque moment'*. But where? That the French Operations Branch of the General Staff was prepared for an attack almost anywhere may be indicated by the fact that the French armour, almost as numerous as the German, was strung out on the whole long front. Its armour did not move in mass opposite the panzer divisions. The French Intelligence Service, which had agents in two of the German panzer divisions,

2 Described further in Chapter 8.

had located some of the panzer in the north. More precise indication of the enemy plan was lacking. Then it fell from the skies in January 1940.

Or did it? Was not this too a plant? The intelligence men at their desks in London frowned and puzzled when they heard the amazing news. A German courier aircraft had landed by mistake in Belgium; the military courier had been arrested and his papers seized nearly intact. What had happened?

There had allegedly been a carouse. A major of the Reserve, whose name is given in German versions as Hoenmanns, flying a fighter aircraft on liaison duties, lost his way on the night of 10 January 1940 when attempting to reach Cologne, and made a forced landing in darkness near Mechelen, on the Meuse. Just as he became aware that he had landed on Belgian territory, his passenger, whom he had taken with him for convenience and against the regulations for courier traffic, revealed that he had alarmingly important papers with him which must be destroyed at all costs. Oddly enough, neither of them carried matches or a lighter.

'*Streichhölzer!*' they shouted to a Belgian forester who first discovered them. He gaped at them. The French or Flemish would have been *Allumettes* or *Lucifer*. Precious moments were lost gesticulating. Hence the appellation that the German Commission of Enquiry gave to it – 'the Lucifer incident'.

Belgian patrols closed in on the aircraft and arrested both officers, posted a guard on the machine, and marched them to a hut where a Belgian officer began the first interrogation. In front of him on the table lay the documents, several sheets headed Air Fleet II, Command Instructions. In one corner glowed an open stove. Suddenly the German courier jumped up, seized the documents and, rushing to the stove, thrust them into it. The Belgian officer, however, no less quickly, snatched the papers from the stove, burning his hands as he did so. The Germans were then placed under stricter guard. The papers were charred, some words lost, but in the main they were still legible.

On 19 January, five days later, Brussels H.Q. recalled all troops from leave, the Dutch Army did the same, and the War Office in London announced that leave was suspended. A Reuter message from Amsterdam stated that a Dutch cabinet meeting had discussed the contents of the captured documents. Meanwhile the German intelligence organisations in Holland and Belgium had been alerted. Colonel Raabe von Pappenheim, German military attaché for Holland and Belgium, has said that Goering had offered a reward of 40,000 Swiss francs for the return of the papers.

The Belgians were puzzled. They wanted to test this amazing case. Would the Germans return willingly to their own country? The German courier officer was sent back to Germany 'to explain matters to his superiors', as Mr Churchill drily remarks.[3] No doubt his reactions were carefully studied as he went. Was he a 'plant'?

The documents were bestowed in a safe within the Belgian Ministry of National Defence. A sentry was posted outside the door of the room. The Belgian government made photostat copies. The Allies studied them.

The charred sheets appeared to be the remains of one of twenty-four numbered copies of instructions to the Second Air Fleet, its Corps, and other Formations; to the 22nd Airborne Infantry Division and its Luftwaffe carrier force; with copies to Army Group B and 6th Army. Whole lines and single words had been burned out and left tantalising gaps. Yet the whole import was clear enough, as the reader can see from the passages that I quote below:

3   *The Second World War*, Vol. ii, *Their Finest Hour*.

3. The German Western Army directs its attack between the North Sea and the Moselle, with the strongest possible airforce support, through the Belgo-Luxembourg region, with the object of . . . . the largest possible groups of its. . . . . The Fortress of Liege and. . . . . surrounded (?). . . . . Further it is intended, with the help of part of the force (10th Army Corps reinforced by 1 Cavalry Division), to seize Dutch territory, with the exception of Festung Holland.

5. *Composition of Army Group B*: see Appendix 2.

6. *Co-operating Forces*:

(a) The 3rd Luftflotte attacks, with all the weight of its aircraft, the French Air Force on the ground, and prevents it from taking part in land operations.

Later it prevents the advance of the French Armies moving north-east from their concentration areas.

The 3rd Luftflotte co-operates also with its Northern Wing (1st Aviation Corps) with Army Group B.

(b) The X Aviation Corps, directly under orders from Air Force Headquarters, operates in close cooperation with the naval forces and the F.d., Luft against the enemy naval forces and, in particular, against the British naval forces.

its reserves. . . . .

With regard to home defence against air attack, the chief object is to protect the ground and war industries organisations.

8. *Forces* – Disposition of the troops and points to be attacked – see Appendix 1.

9. *Reconnaissance.*

(a) Air General Headquarters: reconnaissance to the west of the line Le Havre–Orleans–Bourges–Lyon–Geneva.

(b) 2nd Luftflottes: reconnaissance by Reconnaissance Group 122 to the north-west and west of the line Western Frisian Isles–Amsterdam–Antwerp–Brussels–Nivelles (islands and towns included).

Task:

(a) Find out the disposition of the enemy Air Force in Northern France and Belgium.

(b) Watch the areas where the British Army is concentrated, detect as quickly as possible any movements from that area towards Belgium in the direction of Brussels–Ghent.

Task of the VIII Aviation Corps:

On the first day of the attack, the VIII Aviation Corps supports with part of its forces a landing operation of the VII Aviation Division (see special order).

Closely co-operating with the 6th Army (main action to the west of Maastricht), it supports the advance of the land forces attacking the fortified line and the streams of the basin of the Meuse and destroys the Belgian Army to the west of that region. Attacks against towns and villages during the course of these operations are only permitted if it is *absolutely* certain that they are occupied by troops.

Its fighter squadrons have to obtain command of the air over the area of attack of the 6th Army.

Document 2.

Appreciation of the Situation.

I. Terrain.

On either side of the Meuse a high plateau with heights rising to. . . . . m. Very uneven, in places great differences in height, ravines.

Clayey ground, medium heavy to heavy. Only sparsely (?) populated. The operational area of the Division is on the whole thickly wooded. The Meuse itself constitutes a marked cleft, deeply cut out. Width of river 100m. Banks rising steeply and mainly wooded. Observation very difficult.

Parachute troops can be dropped everywhere in. . . . . the bridges.

Air-borne troops can only be landed at points 15 Km. west of the Meuse on the line Vitrival, M. . . . . Posse.

The country is similar in many respects to that of Freuden. . . . . and troop movements. . . . . not very mobile will be hindered. On the other hand, it lends itself to defence by groups. . . . . widely separated.

What would your reaction be? Would you have 'plumped' for those documents? Would you have hesitated? Think that over before you read further!

In writing of this incident in his memoirs, Mr Churchill says that the 'entire and actual scheme' for the invasion of the West was thus seen and read, but not acted on politically. 'It was argued in all three countries concerned that probably it was a plant.'

Was it? Here we have an insight into the minds that have dwelled too long in the plant house. They eventually can only think round

84

corners, on crooked lines. The men in backroom conferences, far from the little hut at Mechelen, were not well placed to judge the narrow margin by which in the glowing stove those papers were saved from being destroyed altogether. Could that then be a 'plant'?

The trenchant mind of Mr Churchill argued that 'there could be no sense in the Germans trying to make the Belgians believe that they were going to attack them in the near future'. There could be no sense either in thrusting a 'plant' into such a hot stove.

Yet the former French premier, M. Paul Reynaud, in his book *À Cœur Ouvert*, repeats in 1952 the question whether it was not a 'plant', because the dire effect of expert study of the charred sheets was to confirm General Gamelin in his suspicions that the Germans intended a Schlieffen plan form of attack with the weight on the right flank, so increasing Gamelin's faith and emphasis on his counter-plan D, despite the misgivings that Lord Gort had expressed at going so far north to the succour of the neutrals.

We have learned since from General Guderian and Marshal von Manstein that the Lucifer incident, together with reports that the ground was still too soft for panzer, led to postponing the January offensive. Moreover it inclined Hitler and the German High Command of the Army to study Marshal von Manstein's alternative plan for a strong left flank thrust through the Ardennes at Sedan in the rear of the advancing Allied armies. Though not a 'plant', the Lucifer incident was deadly nightshade to the Allies. They took no political action on it; it misled them militarily. Yet the incident was genuine.

So when the Manstein plan was substituted for the plan captured at Mechelen, and its dire surprise revealed in the Ardennes, perhaps the backroom men in London argued that the Mechelen version had in fact been a 'plant'.

I discovered otherwise after the war when I spoke to a former German counter-espionage chief for Holland and Belgium, Lt.-Cdr.

Richard Protze (Uncle Richard) who worked under cover between 1938 and 1940 in Holland, posing as Herr Paarmann, the manager of the Reich Railways Travel Office in the Hague.

'Hitler managed his own deception at that time,' he said. 'How could the staff here do any strategic deception planning, when it was unaware what Hitler would order next? I was told to get those Mechelen papers back at any cost, because they were genuine. Our military attaché for the Hague and Brussels, Colonel Raabe von Pappenheim, told me that Goering offered 40,000 Swiss francs for the documents.'

This seemed to me pretty conclusive that the Mechelen documents were genuine. I looked across at Lieutenant-Commander Richard Protze, alias Herr Paarmann, alias Uncle Richard, and asked him about plant life in Germany. Were plants officially cultivated in the Third Reich? The old man, when I met him in Holstein, looked back at me with watery blue eyes, eyes in which the hypnotic stare that he had used in countless interrogations was still not wholly extinguished, and being about the eldest surviving member of the former German intelligence service, he felt himself entitled to discourse on the history of the plant.

Yes, of course we dealt in plants. Blossoms we called them – Blüten – and many is the plant that I have watered and helped to grow. The business came under Branch III of the Abwehr – that is counter-espionage and security – and we divided it into two sections, III D and III F. The officers of Section III D had to manufacture the plants. They were 'fed' with Allied requirements by III F, and III F in turn took delivery of the documents, or the answers, and saw that they reached the Allies in one way or another. If the French wanted to know the composition of our armoured divisions, why then, they must be told what was least dangerous for them to know!

The production section III D had to discuss every piece of deception with the appropriate branch of the General Staff or the Naval Staff. It had to be worked out exactly what the foreign powers might be told and what they might not be told. Sometimes we exaggerated, but more usually we understated. As long as the deception held, we were tying down enemy agents without giving away vital material. Sometimes the French General Staff would see through our material, and bitter recriminations would follow. An agent would be removed. The game would start again, the hunt would be resumed between intelligence officers and counter-intelligence officers, and agents moving to and fro between them.

It was in that way that I once supplied to the French Intelligence Service the formula for the resistant qualities in the armour plating of our new pocket battleships. We called it 'Caniron'. Our naval construction experts worked out a formula with immense care. Unfortunately the French were not inclined to trust the formula entirely and they managed to secure a piece of the armour plate as well from one of our dockyards. The characteristics of this armour plate were altogether different from those of the Caniron formula. A painful scene followed between myself and one of the French intelligence officers in Holland, Captain Lataudrie. He would not even shake hands on parting. That is what happens when a plant is discovered. It breaks up old friendships.

But the plant, my friend, is often a great deal of trouble, and we only used it to prevent enemy agents from getting to the real thing. We did not plant just for the sake of planting. Occasionally too we used the plant to lead us to the other enemy agents and discover the real leakages in our own security. Let me give you an example!

In the early 1930s, we suspected that the Poles in Berlin were informed of the most secret strategic and technical planning of the Reichswehr. We thought that they were obtaining documents from the Reichswehr Ministry itself. So I used the plant system to discover which section of the Reichswehr Ministry was involved. This is how I did it. I knew of a Polish intelligence officer in Berlin whose heart was not in his job. He often came to us for information and did not care whether it was genuine or not. So I gave him certain specially prepared plants that he would have to photograph quickly and return. By that means, he got access at odd hours to the dark room in the grounds of the Polish Embassy and so was able to read and memorise the reference numbers on other photographs of German documents hung up on the drying boards by another Polish intelligence officer. As soon as we had the information that we wanted, we began to stop supplying those plants. It is never good to be discovered at that. Plants should be used with care.

'What about leaving documents in taxicabs?' I asked.

The old man chuckled.

'As old as the hills,' he said. 'Tell me another.'

'And what about leaving documents in desks and dressing-rooms – the forgetful ambassador act?'

'That might be a "plant" too – though less likely.'

'And stupid couriers?' I asked.

'I know the trick of the stupid courier,' the old man answered. 'There is not much that you can tell me.'

It was on the tip of my tongue to ask: 'And what about the dead courier?' but I restrained my curiosity; for at that time I was not certain that the case of Major Martin would ever see the light of day in all detail.

What a pity that Uncle Richard died before the full hoax was revealed! How he would have laughed!

This catalogue of plants is by no means exhaustive. I have taken a few specimens at random, and shown moreover that the real thing can be mistaken for a plant. In such an atmosphere as this, the intelligence officer can often lose his sense of proportion. Suspicion is an occupational disease. If he slips on a banana skin he suspects a plant; if the valet mislays his solitaires he suspects that he is an enemy agent frustrating a vital appointment; if a man at the next table as much as looks over the top of the wine list, he asks for his table to be changed. He looks under his bed, he examines his writing desk to see if any paper has been shifted. He forgets that he shifted it himself! At this stage, plant life has got the better of him, and retirement is recommended. Real gardening somewhere in the country!

That is, however, a stage beyond the immediate search. We have established that plants are used by every military power that has something to hide. We are searching now for the origins of the strangest plant of all, and so I return you to the real thing via the Mechelen incident.

In the years after the French and British armies had been flung back and evacuated from Dunkirk, the boys in the backrooms and basements of Whitehall had plenty of time to reflect whether it was a plant or the real thing that had dropped from the skies on Mechelen. Whatever conclusion they came to, obviously the setting was good enough to serve for a plant some time in the future, when we would take the initiative. An aircraft accident, a hapless courier, a set of operational orders, partly destroyed! The ingredients of a 'plant' were there certainly! Strange and more exotic growths would be necessary to satisfy the enemy taste. Imagination and artistry would be needed.

8
MEETING THE HUSH MEN

So far I had found a grave and the sight of some documents had been promised to me; but I was still without a positive clue to how the idea of using a dead body had come into the minds of the living. I met Julian again one day, who congratulated me on my search in Spain, but when I spoke of wanting to find the man who had the idea, Julian shook his head.

'There are some pretty queer birds underground in Whitehall,' he said. 'If they are still in the Show, they cannot talk. Even when they are retired from the Show, they cannot talk either – not the regular men. At least I've never known them do that.'

But I burrowed and delved, asked questions of war correspondents and colleagues of the press who had been on temporary duties with the intelligence services in wartime, and at length a meeting was fixed with some hush men who might answer a few questions that were puzzling me.

In the meantime, I looked over the principal combined operations of the war in the west, and saw that there had been a steady improvement in the surprise element as the war progressed. Evidently the technique of cover plan and deception had been more seriously studied as months went by. These were my findings:

Dakar, September 1940. This raid on West Africa was made so soon after Dunkirk, while our military effort was still disorganised, that the technique of security and deception could not be fully employed. There was the complication that Admiral Darlan, smarting under the memory of Oran and the loss of some other warships to the British, had put his intelligence service at the disposal of the Germans. General de Gaulle in London had to initiate many Free French officers into the secrets of the Dakar operation to get their allegiance. The landing craft taking part in the operation were carried overland to Liverpool on trailers serviced by troops in tropical kit. At Liverpool, there was a dinner party of ardent French officers with a toast of *à Dakar*!

There appears to have been no cover plan. Mr Churchill reveals that a letter from the Foreign Secretary, which he read to the Chiefs of Staff Committee on 22 August, disclosed a leakage of information. Delay made it more likely that the leakage would eventually reach the Germans. In one way and another, surprise at Dakar was lost. Referring to attempts to disguise the operation, Mr Churchill wrote: 'Such forms of "cover" were carried to remarkable refinements as we became more experienced and wily.'[4]

Dieppe, August 1942. This was the largest of the Channel raids, Operation 'Jubilee'. It had been postponed once, which inevitably leads to a relaxing of security. Planning officers argued that if there had been a previous leakage, the postponement might have allayed

4   *The Second World War*, Vol. ii, *Their Finest Hour.*

German suspicions. Usually, however, a leakage that reaches the enemy leads to prolonged vigilance.

An intriguing advertisement in British newspapers for a soap product appeared a few days before the operation with frequent references to the advisability of washing 'that Beach Coat from Dieppe' in a certain brand of flakes.

This puzzling advertisement and small traces of security breaches had brought officers of Combined Operations Headquarters into a high lather; but the Chief of Combined Operations, Admiral Lord Louis Mountbatten, wisely ignored the advertisement altogether. To make enquiries as to its origin might have started a new leakage altogether. The operation went ahead.

'Our post-war examination of their records,' wrote Mr Churchill, 'shows that the Germans did not receive through leakages of information any special warning of our intention to attack.'

Dieppe was an improvement on Dakar. The heavy casualties at Dieppe were not due to lack of surprise.

The North African landings, 7–8 November 1942, Operation 'Torch'. This time the convoys were so large that an elaborate cover plan was certainly needed. 'Secrecy can only be maintained by deception,' wrote the 'Former Naval Person' to President Roosevelt on 27 July 1942, explaining that he intended to hold several irons in the fire to keep the enemy guessing. The American troops sailing in General Eisenhower's convoys would, on being served out with tropical kit, hear it said that they were drafts for Basra or Suez. Meanwhile, Canadian troops in Great Britain would be issued with Arctic clothing!

Deception was to go much further than that. The convoys sailing from the Clyde were this time said to be bound for Dakar. The large fleet assembling at Gibraltar with strange new landing-craft was rumoured to be bound for Malta to relieve the hard-pressed

George Cross island, or to force its way to Alexandria and reinforce General Alexander by the dangerous Mediterranean route. Skilfully, the naval intelligence officers in Gibraltar planted the rumours on those same men among the Spanish dockyard labourers whom they suspected of being in touch with the Abwehr villa in Algeciras across the bay. No doubt among the throng of Spanish and German intelligence officers who frequented the Reina Maria Cristina hotel, the same reports were sown at the bar and across the tables. In Madrid there were means at the disposal of the British attachés. Even certain high Spanish officers were said to be involved in placing the misleading information.

What was the result this time? The false reports smothered the true. I have personal assurance both from Captain Wilhelm Lenz, senior German intelligence officer in Spain, and from Joacquim Canaris that some German Military Intelligence officers forecast the correct destination for 'Torch'.

'I told the head of the Naval branch of the Abwehr when he visited Madrid,' said Lenz. 'Lieutenant Canaris sent a ciphered message by radio from Madrid early in November that an attack on North Africa was imminent.'

Yet we know that Admiral Canaris had to report personally to a furious Hitler after Operation 'Torch' had begun and take with him a bundle of intelligence reports alleging that he had indeed forecast the North African landings. He also made excuses to Goebbels! 'Admiral Canaris gave me a verbal report on the work of our intelligence service,' wrote Goebbels on 9 April 1943.

> I gather that it has done better than I assumed. Unfortunately the results of its work were mishandled. Thus, for instance, our espionage reported the North African venture of the British and Americans as well as the meeting in Casablanca well

beforehand; but these facts were not reported to the Führer
sufficiently clearly.[5]

How many other and contradictory reports were there as well?
Nobody likes to admit to mistakes afterwards. But Sir Samuel
Hoare described how the Ribbentrop intelligence organisation was
deceived. Dr von Stohrer at dinner on the day before the operation
spoke his conviction to Spanish naval officers that the convoys
were destined for Malta or Alexandria, nor could the Spaniards per-
suade the German ambassador to the contrary.[6]

We have the evidence of Lieutenant von Schlabrendorff that

in the first days of November 1942, when the German Naval
Command reported that a strong Allied convoy protected by
men-of-war had passed through the Straits of Gibraltar steering
an eastward course, General von Tresckow inquired of General
Heusinger, Chief of Operations in the Army High Command,
what this might portend, and received Heusinger's reply: 'We are
convinced that this is an attempt by the Allies to relieve the island
of Malta, which is being heavily battered. No landing in North
Africa is to be apprehended. The British and Americans lack the
forces and the experience for such an enterprise.'[7]

Better and better; but there could not be yet another success in strategic deception unless new methods were used. Those agents who
had helped carry on our 'plant' warfare would be suspect at least.
Certain prolific channels of deceit would be dammed now. There
would be reproaches and protestations, and some good friends

5   *The Goebbels Diaries*, p. 246.
6   *Ambassador on Special Mission.*
7   *Revolt Against Hitler.*

would part. By what new trick would we disguise our thrust at the soft underbelly of the beast?

The hush men met me with an air of reticence. They were a group who together produced an atmosphere of precision and acuteness that augurs well for intelligence work. We sat in arm-chairs and talked.

'Did the idea just come out of the blue?' I asked, 'or had it some foundation?'

'It was based on real operations.'

'Was it connected at all with the Mechelen aircraft incident?'

'Well, that was studied, and for a long time we thought that the Mechelen incident might be a plant. But there was another operation in the First World War – Allenby in Palestine. Study Wavell's book and you will find what was called the "haversack" ruse.'

'There were quite a number of you people who were "friends" of Major Martin?' I asked. 'Did it take you long to get official approval for the operation with a body?'

'No, it really went through more quickly than we expected.'

'Do you know who the man really was?'

'No. Sir Bernard Spilsbury came into this operation, as you may know; but it is unlikely that you will find anything in his papers.'

Sir Bernard Spilsbury – the great pathologist who committed suicide in 1947 and left behind him a meticulous card index of every corpse he had ever handled. Had he been asked to find a body? It has already been related that he was unofficial adviser to the secret ser-vice men who were preparing the operation.

One of them talked of Sicily on the eve of the operation. He spoke of Prince Umberto making a tour of inspection in a comic opera atmosphere of Allied bombs falling and Italian officers hid-ing in Sicilian orange groves and wine vaults. He seemed to think that the Italians had not felt that they were directly threatened by an invasion of Sicily, though obviously with such bombing they could hardly feel secure.

Next day I turned up Wavell's biography of Allenby and found the haversack ruse. General Lord Wavell related this of the campaign of October–November 1917, which brought the third battle of Gaza. Allenby facing north in the coastal plain was bent on driving back the Turks and Germans, who threatened Suez.

'The steps taken to deceive the Turk were varied and ingenious,' wrote Wavell;

> the most spectacular was the famous haversack ruse in which a staff officer contrived to be chased by the Turkish outposts, pretended to be wounded and dropped, with other articles, a haversack stained with fresh blood containing papers, letters, money. The papers and letters had been very skilfully prepared, firstly to give the impression that they were genuine and secondly to convey the impression that the main attack was coming at Gaza, and that the preparations at Beersheba were only a feint. It is now known that these papers were one of the principal influences that determined the action of the Turks before and during the battle. But it was only one of the many steps taken to conceal the real plan, and to implant a fictitious reading of it in the minds of the enemy.[8]

The Official History was even more explicit and gave the whole scope of the deception work at the time with curious frankness, considering that it was an official work and some squeamishness is often felt at revealing our secret technique.

'The main operation then depended on the speedy capture of

8   p. 202 of *Allenby – A Study in Greatness*, by General Sir Archibald Wavell. George G. Harrap & Co.

Beersheba with its water supply, and all subsequent movements hinged upon the success of this first,' wrote the official historians.[9]

Several ruses were employed to deceive the enemy. One, which may be described as strategic, was an endeavour to make the Turks believe that a landing on the northern coast of Syria, probably on the gulf of Iskanderun, would be attempted from Cyprus. Sites for camps were laid out on the island, and as much stir as possible made by garrison troops. Bogus messages were dispatched by wireless and enquiries made of contractors regarding the provision of rations on a considerable scale. Docks and wharves were labelled for the embarkation and disembarkation of troops and stores and reports circulated that it was proposed to form a base on the island.

This ruse does not appear to have had any success. But another of a very much simpler nature was to have an extraordinary effect, an effect indeed hardly to be matched in the annals of modern war. An officer of the Staff at G.H.Q. rode out into No Man's Land on 10 October 1917, accompanied by a small escort, as if on reconnaissance. Near El Girheir on the bank of the Wadi Hanafish he was fired on by a Turkish cavalry patrol, which then gave chase.

He pretended to be wounded, rolled about in the saddle, finally dropped field glasses and other articles, including a bundle of papers in a haversack, which he had previously stained with fresh blood from his horse. Having ascertained that a Turkish trooper had picked up the papers, he made his escape. The most important papers in the portfolio were mock agenda for a conference at G.H.Q. indicating that the main attack would be carried out against Gaza, accompanied by a landing on the coast north of

9   *Official History of the Palestine Campaign*, Vol. i, p. 312.

the town with subsidiary operations by mounted troops against Beersheba, more or less as a feint; together with G.H.Q. instructions for the above attack. There were also a few rough notes on a cipher, sufficient to enable an expert on cipher work to decode any dummy messages that might be sent out by wireless later on. Other private documents were so cleverly faked that they greatly heightened the effect of the principal ones.[10]

After the capture of Gaza, an order was found signed by Colonel Ali Fuad Bey commanding the Turkish XX Corps stating that he had rewarded the N.C.O. in charge of the patrol which had obtained such valuable information, and warning his own officers against carrying papers when they were on reconnaissance. But before that happened, the effect of the ruse was seen. Work on trenches immediately decreased on the enemy's left and was greatly increased on his right. The enemy was deceived and the deception had a very important effect upon his plans.[11]

Indeed the German commander of the Eighth German–Turkish Army, General Baron Kress von Kressenstein, examined the haversack papers himself and 'while not overlooking the possibility that they were faked, he inclined strongly to believe in their authenticity'.

10 Twenty pounds in notes were included to give the impression that the loss was not intentional. There were personal letters from home of a type which it might be expected the recipient would not willingly lose. There was a private letter from an imaginary staff officer indicating that the main attack would be on Gaza and frankly criticising the obtuseness of G.H.Q. in not operating against the other flank. There was also the copy of a telegram from G.H.Q. to Desert Mounted Corps stating that a staff officer was going out on patrol towards El Girheir. A few days later a notice was inserted in Desert Corps orders that a notebook had been lost and that the finder was to return it to G.H.Q. A party was sent out to search for it, and the officer in command threw away some sandwiches wrapped up in a copy of the orders on the approach of the enemy.
11 'The officer who planned and carried out this ruse had requested that his name should not be made public, and though it is well known not only in the British army but to the Turks, it has seemed reasonable to comply with his desire.' [Original footnote.]

Kress was removed from command of the Eighth Army next spring – 'it appears that he had forfeited the confidence of senior Turkish officers as a result of his dispositions at the third battle of Gaza and his failure to anticipate that the main British attack would come on the Turkish left'.

So we had drawn off the Turkish strength towards the coast before we struck inland.

Such was the official account. Sir George Aston in his book *Secret Service* actually printed the love letter, specially written to heighten the colour of the other documents in the haversack.

36 Balham Gardens,
London, S.W.
August 21st, 1917.

DEAREST,

How I wish you were here now! I am simply longing for you and would love to show you our dear little baby son. I am so proud of him. He is such a splendid little fellow and so good.

You must not worry about either of us, as I get stronger every day and baby, the doctor says, could not be better. Richard is the name we are giving him – I know it is the one that you always had in mind, and I chose it as I felt you would be glad I had remembered it. All your sisters came and Alice wanted to adopt him at once.

I sent you a telegram as soon as baby was born, and your reply arrived three days later. If it had been you arriving instead of the telegram how lovely it would have been. Darling you *must* try to come and see your little son. Don't smile if I say that to me he already has a look of you. He is such a darling and you will love him so.

I heard the last raid but no bombs were thrown anywhere near. Poor baby! Fancy coming into the world to find this awful war going on and Germans dropping bombs all over London. Louis had a narrow escape in the office; for some of his windows were broken.

Good-bye, my darling – Nurse says I must not tire myself by writing too much – so no more now but I will write again soon and then it will be a longer letter than this. Take care of your precious self! All my love and many kisses.

Your loving wife,

MARY
Baby sends a kiss to Daddy.

You can see the chintz curtains and the pink-rose complexioned mother of First World War days who would have written such a letter. Only one phrase jarred on my critical sense, and Kress von Kressenstein must have overlooked it in his rapture.

'I sent you a telegram as soon as baby was born and your reply arrived three days later.' 'A telegram' was wrong, when he had already received it. That should have read:

'My telegram was sent as soon as baby was born and yours reached me three days later.'

A small point, no doubt, but in this deception, the finest point might tell. So the ruse had already been practised at least once already by a living man. That ruse had moreover been described in the British Official History of the War, in Wavell's *Allenby*, in Sir George Aston's *Secret Service* and in Captain Ferdinand Tuohy's *The Secret Corps*. All these books were most probably to be found in the library of the German General Staff, and certainly the German

Army must have studied the incident. The next time a haversack ruse was tried, it would have to be superlatively good.

Of that much the heads of the British intelligence were certain themselves, because although they were intrigued by this brilliant idea of the deception boys, they warned that it had a dangerous drawback. If there was one detail wrong which the Germans detected, then the deception would turn out to be a top leakage. The whole Allied strategy for the next blow in the Mediterranean would be laid bare.

Yes, it would have to be a superlatively good operation.

9
SEEING THE EVIDENCE

So the armies closed on Tunisia, and President Roosevelt met Mr Churchill in Casablanca, the rendezvous that Captain Lenz's listen-girl in the cafes of Madrid had mistaken for a codeword for the 'White House', and in January 1943 the two statesmen decided upon the next thrust at the underbelly of the beast. It was to be Sicily. From that moment onwards the field was open for the cover plan. Although it was by no means all contained in the scope of Major Martin's last journey, that is the part of the deception plan that has been released for publication, and that we can examine to our heart's content in all but a few significant details.

There had to be first an outline plan, and then a body to fit the plan. It had been, as already related, Sir Bernard Spilsbury the pathologist who advised on the use of a body, on the appearance and condition of a drowned body, and possibly also on the most likely way in which a body could be procured. Thereafter a name was sought for the operation, and the name Operation 'Mincemeat' was given to it. It has been explained by Lieutenant-Commander Ewen Montagu,[12] who at this time was very actively employed at the London end of the operation, that this name was simply the next on the list of cover names supplied by the Admiralty.

I find that an odd explanation, since neither Operation 'Overlord', 'Sledgehammer', 'Husky' nor any other important codename came off a list. Each name was invented by the planners, passed by the Security officers and listed afterwards.

It has also been stated that the right body was found at the right moment, and that by great good fortune the parents of the body were willing to give assent to that body being used in a secret operation. I have no other explanation to offer for this readily available body, and I therefore recommend the readers to accept the facts as they are presented.

In two folders neatly ordered, the evidence in the case of Operation 'Mincemeat' was presented to me, the one of documents stained and worn by exposure to salt water, the other more legible – photo-copies of the documents before they were put in the dead man's pockets and sent with him on his last journey.

I am laying this evidence before the reader, who may assume the reactions of a puzzled Spanish naval officer or a suspicious German intelligence officer when the papers came eventually to be opened. But it is first necessary to read those papers upon which Operation 'Mincemeat' was planned before examining what was found on the body.

---

12 *The Man Who Never Was.* The Hon. Ewen S. Montagu, Q.C., Sunday Express Series of Articles, 1953.

MOST SECRET

Operation Mincemeat

OBJECT. To place in the hands of the enemy documents which will lead them to believe that the target of the next attack by the Allies is the cover target.

METHOD OF IMPLEMENTATION. To cause a body dressed in military uniform to drift ashore in Spain, as if from an aircraft en route to A.F.H.Q. North Africa. It is anticipated that enemy agents will obtain the documents with the body (or copies of them) and hand them over to the Germans.

PRESENT POSITION. Arrangements are being made to see that no leakage occurs in Spain of the fact that this is a 'plant'. The body is available and minor matters are being catered for.

POINTS FOR DECISION.

1. It will be necessary to place the body in the water close inshore somewhere in the neighbourhood of Cadiz at a time when there is an onshore wind. (According to the Hydrographic Dept. the prevailing tidal streams alone will not bring the body ashore.)

2. It is undesirable, for security reasons, to mount this operation from Gibraltar.

3. In those circumstances there seem to be four possible ways of placing the body (with some wreckage and a rubber dinghy) in the water:

(a) by surface ship (an escort of a convoy)

(b) by submarine

(c) by land aircraft

(d) by flying boat.

4.　(a) A surface ship is not considered possible owing to the need for placing the body, etc., close inshore and the need for choosing a time with an onshore wind.

(b) A submarine would necessitate using a rubber dinghy to take the body, etc., close enough inshore. It would be the ideal method from the point of view of choosing the right time for wind conditions. There would be technical difficulties in keeping the body fresh during the passage: in a surface ship it could be kept in a container with 'dry ice' but this would release carbon dioxide which would be unacceptable in a submarine. It might be possible to arrange some form of suitable storage outside the pressurehull and if transport by submarine is decided on, this point should be investigated. After the body had been planted it would help the illusion if a 'set piece' giving a flare and explosion with delay-action fuse could be left to give the impression of an aircraft crash.

(c) A land aircraft could take off when Met. reports suggested the right conditions, but if the body were dropped in this way it might be smashed to pieces on landing.

(d) A flying boat could take off in accordance with weather conditions. The most convincing procedure would be for the aircraft to come in from out at sea simulating engine trouble, drop a bomb to simulate the crash, go out to sea as quickly as possible, return (as if it were a second flying boat) and drop a flare as if searching for the first aircraft, land, and then, while ostensibly searching for survivors, drop the body, etc., and then take off again.

5. It is suggested that, of these methods, a submarine is the best (if the necessary preservation of the body can be achieved) and a flying boat the next best.

6. It is requested that a decision be obtained from the appropriate authority as to which method should be used, so that arrangements can be made.

The name of the officer who drew up this plan has not been revealed, probably for security reasons. It was expanded into a more detailed plan by the naval officer in charge of carrying out the operation, Lt.-Cdr. Montagu, who went into the various considerations attaching to security, and the most realistic presentation of the corpse and its belongings.

A large insulated metal container was designed to take Major Martin out of the United Kingdom, and the intelligence officers settled down to producing the highly delicate documents that would convey to the enemy the false picture of our Mediterranean strategy. They also produced the hardly less important papers that were to give this nameless corpse the appearance of a dead staff officer fresh from London with important dispatches.

Here then is a list of his personal belongings:

CLOTHING

1 vest
1 pants

1 shirt, khaki
1 tie
1 pr. socks, khaki
1 pr. socks, heavy grey woollen
1 pr. sock suspenders
1 pr. braces
1 blouse, battle-dress { metal crown
khaki { cloth 'Royal Marines' flash
{ C. C. O. badge
1 pr. trousers, battle-dress khaki
1 handkerchief, khaki
1 handkerchief, white
1 trench-coat, metal crown and 'R.M.'
1 glove
1 pr. boots
1 pr. gaiters
1 'Mae West' life-jacket

PERSONAL DOCUMENTS
AND ARTICLES IN POCKETS

Identity discs (2) 'Major W. MARTIN, R.M., R/C' attached
    to braces
Silver cross on silver chain round neck Watch, wrist
Wallet, containing:
        photograph of fiancée
        book of stamps (2 used)
        2 letters from fiancée
        St Christopher plaque
        Invitation to Cabaret Club

C.C.O. pass
Admiralty identity card } In cellophane container

Torn off top of letter

1 £5 note – 5 March 1942, C227 45827

3 £1 notes X 34D 527008, W 21D 029293, X 66D 443119

1 half-crown

2 shillings

2 sixpences

4 pennies

Letter from 'Father'

Letter from 'Father' to Solicitors

Letter from Lloyds Bank

Bill (receipted) from Naval and Military Club

Bill (cash) from Gieves, Ltd.

Bill for engagement ring

2 bus tickets

2 counterfoil stubs of tickets for Prince of Wales Theatre 22. 4. 43

Box of matches

Packet of cigarettes

Bunch of keys

Pencil stub

Letter from Solicitors

These exhibits seem to be trivial details beside the War Office letter signed by the Vice Chief of Imperial General Staff, General Sir Archibald Nye, and addressed to General Sir Harold Alexander, Commander-in-Chief of 80th Army Group at Algiers; or the supporting letter from Rear-Admiral Lord Louis Mountbatten, Chief of Combined Operations. These are the only documents that Captain Lenz sent in copy to Berlin, so let us read them first.

MY DEAR ALEX—

I am taking advantage of sending you a personal letter by hand of one of Mountbatten's officers, to give you the inside history of our recent exchange of cables about Mediterranean operations and their attendant cover plans. You may have felt our decisions were somewhat arbitrary, but I can assure you in fact that the C.O.S. Committee gave the most careful consideration both to your recommendation and also to Jumbo's.[13]

We have had recent information that the Bosche have been reinforcing and strengthening their defences in Greece and Crete and C.I.G.S. felt that our forces for the assault were insufficient. It was agreed by the Chiefs of Staff that the 5th Division should be reinforced by one brigade group for the assault on the beach south of Cape Araxos and that a similar reinforcement should be made for the 56th Division at Kalamata. We are earmarking the necessary forces and shipping.

Jumbo Wilson had proposed to select Sicily as cover target for 'Husky'; but we have already chosen it as cover for Operation 'Brimstone'.

The C.O.S. Committee went into the whole question exhaustively again and came to the conclusion that in view of the preparations in Algeria, the amphibious training which will be taking place on the Tunisian coast and the heavy air bombardment which will be put down to neutralise the Sicilian airfields, we should stick to our plan of making it cover for 'Brimstone' – indeed we stand a very good chance of making him think we will go for Sicily – it is an obvious objective and one about which he must be nervous.

On the other hand, they felt there wasn't much hope of persuading the Bosche that the extensive preparations in the Eastern

---

13 Nickname for General (later Field-Marshal) Wilson. [Author's footnote.]

Mediterranean were also directed at Sicily. For this reason they have told Wilson his cover plan should be something nearer the spot, e.g. the Dodecanese. Since our relations with Turkey are now so obviously closer the Italians must be pretty apprehensive about these islands.

I imagine you will agree with these arguments. I know you will have your hands more than full at the moment and you haven't much chance of discussing future operations with Eisenhower. But if by any chance you do want to support Wilson's proposal I hope you will let us know soon, because we can't delay much longer.

I am very sorry we weren't able to meet your wishes about the new commander of the Guards Brigade. Your own nominee was down with a bad attack of 'flu and not likely to be really fit for another few weeks. No doubt, however, you know Forster personally; he has done extremely well in command of a brigade at home, and is, I think, the best fellow available.

You must be about as fed up as we are with the whole question of war medals and 'Purple Hearts'. We all agree with you that we don't want to offend our American friends, but there is a good deal more to it than that. If our troops who happen to be serving in one particular theatre are to get extra decorations merely because the Americans happen to be serving there too, we will be faced with a good deal of discontent among those troops fighting elsewhere perhaps just as bitterly – or more so. My own feeling is that we should thank the Americans for their kind offer but say firmly it would cause too many anomalies and we are sorry we can't accept. But it is on the agenda for the next Military Members meeting and I hope you will have a decision very soon.

Best of luck

Yours ever

ARCHIE NYE.

On choice blue official paper, the letter of Mountbatten read:

Combined Operations Headquarters,
1 A, Richmond Terrace,
Whitehall, S.W.1.
April 21st, 1943.

DEAR ADMIRAL OF THE FLEET,[14]

I promised V.C.I.G.S. that Major Martin would arrange with you for the onward transmission of a letter he has with him for General Alexander.

It is very urgent and very 'hot' and as there are some remarks in it that could not be seen by others in the War Office, it could not go by signal. I feel sure that you will see that it goes on safely and without delay.

I think you will find Martin the man you want.

He is quiet and shy at first, but he really knows his stuff. He was more accurate than some of us about the probable run of events at Dieppe and he has been well in on the experiments with the latest barges and equipment which took place up in Scotland.

Let me have him back, please, as soon as the assault is over. He might bring some sardines with him – they are 'on points' here![15]

Yours sincerely
LOUIS MOUNTBATTEN.

Briefly then, the official documents suggest that the British Chiefs of Staff are worried by German troop concentrations in Greece which may make an assault there more difficult.

14   Admiral of the Fleet Sir Andrew Cunningham, C. in C. Mediterranean.
15   A veiled allusion to Sardinia. [Author's footnotes.]

They propose moreover that feint attacks, mostly by air, shall be made on Sicily in order to distract the Axis from another main target – not named but probably Sardinia – for what else could the Allies attack on the soft underbelly but Sardinia, Sicily, the toe of Italy or Greece? Having read important conclusions out of those two letters, what would the enemy intelligence officer do, but ask for fuller details about the accident that brought them into his hands?

Who was this drowned officer? If he was already buried, what proof remained of his identity? To satisfy their curiosity, the whole range of exhibits existed, and by unfolding the sodden discoloured personal letters the intelligence officer could get a better idea of the kind of man that Major Martin had been.

The Manor House,
Ogbourne St. George,
Marlborough,
Wiltshire.
Sunday 18th.

I do think, dearest, that seeing people like you off at railway stations is one of the poorer forms of sport. A train going out can leave a howling great gap in one's life and one has to try madly – and quite in vain – to fill it with all the things one used to enjoy a whole five weeks ago. That lovely golden day we spent together – oh! I know it's been said before, but if <u>only</u> time would sometimes stand still just for a <u>minute.</u> But that line of thought is too pointless. Pull your socks up Pam and don't be a silly little fool.

Your letter made me feel slightly better – but I shall get horribly conceited if you go on saying things like that about me – they're utterly unlike ME, as I'm afraid you'll soon find out. Here I am for the week-end in this divine place with Mummy and Jane being too sweet and understanding the whole time, bored beyond words and panting for Monday so that I can get back to the old grindstone again. What an idiotic waste!

Bill darling, do let me know as soon as you get fixed and can make some more plans, and don't <u>please</u> let them send you off into the blue the horrible way they do nowadays – now that we've found each other out of the whole world, don't think I could bear it—

All my love,
PAM.

Office, Wednesday 21st.

The Bloodhound has left his kennel for half an hour so here I am scribbling nonsense to you again. Your letter came this morning just as I was dashing out – madly late as usual! You do write such heavenly ones. But what are these horrible dark hints you're throwing out about being sent off somewhere – <u>of course</u> I won't say a word to anyone – I never do when you tell me things, but it's not abroad is it? Because I won't have it. I <u>won't,</u> tell them so from me. Darling, why did we go and meet in the middle of a war, such a silly thing for anybody to do – if it weren't for the war we might have been nearly married by now, going round together choosing curtains etc and I wouldn't be sitting in a dreary Government office typing idiotic minutes all day long – I <u>know</u> the futile sort of work I do doesn't make the war one minute shorter.

Dearest Bill, I'm so thrilled with my ring – scandalously extravagant – you know how I adore diamonds – I simply can't stop looking at it.

I'm going to a rather dreary dance tonight with Jock and Hazel. I think they've got some other man coming. You know what their friends always turn out to be like, he'll have the sweetest little Adam's apple and the shiniest bald head! How beastly and ungrateful of me, but it isn't really that – you know – don't you?

Look darling, I've got next Sunday and Monday off for Easter. I shall go home for it of course, <u>do</u> come too if you possibly can, or even if you can't get away from London I'll dash up and we'll have an evening of gaiety – (By the way Aunt Marian said to bring you to dinner next time I was up, but I think that might wait?)

Here comes the Bloodhound, masses of love and a kiss
from
PAM.

Two love letters, and then a paternal letter from his father, enclosing another letter from the family solicitors.

13 April 1943.

MY DEAR WILLIAM,
I cannot say that this hotel is any longer as comfortable[16] as remember it to have been in pre-war days. I am, however, staying here as the only alternative to imposing myself once more upon your aunt, whose depleted staff and strict regard for fuel economy (which I agree to be necessary in war time) has made the house almost uninhabitable to a guest, at least one of my age.

I propose to be in Town for the nights of the 20th and 21st of April when no doubt we shall have an opportunity to meet. I enclose the copy of a letter which I have written to Gwatkin of McKenna's (his solicitor) about your affairs. You will see that

16 Unless in the black market for food, fuel and labour, no hotel was as comfortable in 1943 as it had been in pre-war days! [Author's footnote.]

I have asked him to lunch with me at the Carlton Grill (which I understand still to be open) at a quarter to one on Wednesday the 21st. I should be glad if you would make it possible to join us. We shall not however wait luncheon for you, so I trust that, if you are able to come, you will make a point of being punctual.

Your cousin Priscilla has asked to be remembered to you. She has grown into a sensible girl though I cannot say that her work for the Land Army has done much to improve her looks. In that respect I am afraid that she will take after her father's side of the family.

Your affectionate
FATHER.

Then there was a letter from Lloyds Bank, which every citizen will read with sympathy:

14 April, 1943.
Private.
Major W. Martin, R.M.,
Army and Navy Club, Pall Mall,
London, S.W.1.

DEAR SIR,
I am given to understand that in spite of repeated application your overdraft amounting to £79 19s. 2d. still outstands.

In the circumstances, I am now writing to inform you that unless this amount, plus interest at 4% to date of payment, is received forthwith we shall have no alternative but to take the necessary steps to protect our interests.
Yours faithfully,
[signed]

and a letter to Major William Martin, who had apparently just made his will, from the family solicitors:

19 April 1943.

DEAR SIR,
re your affairs
We thank you for your letter of yesterday's date returning the draft of your will approved. We will insert the legacy of £50 to your batman and our Mr. Gwatkin will bring the fair copy with him when he meets you at lunch on the 21st inst. so that you can sign it there.

The inspector of taxes has asked us for particulars of your service pay and allowances during 1941–2 before he will finally agree to the amount of reliefs due to you for that year. We cannot find that we have ever had these particulars and shall, therefore, be grateful if you will let us have them.
Yours faithfully,
[signed]

MAJOR W. MARTIN, R.M.,
Naval and Military Club,
94, Piccadilly,
London, W.1.

Out of tunic and trousers pockets there would be taken, smoothed and dried, a bill from the Naval and Military Club, a paid bill with Gieves the naval tailors for a shirt and three collars, an identity card, a membership card to the Cabaret Club, a photograph of a rather dishevelled girl drying herself on the beach with a bath towel, a valid pass to Combined Operations Headquarters, an expired pass to the same building, two stubs of tickets for a musical show *Strike a New Note* at the Prince of Wales Theatre, a jeweller's bill for £53 for an engagement ring, and a bus ticket.

That exhausts the documentary evidence that Major William Martin, Royal Marines, really existed, created out of an unnamed corpse by several ingenious officers. The reader may well reflect on this evidence, and ask whether there is any flaw in it.

For my taste the letters are too explicit. How seldom is it that people in close sympathy of mind need to round off their phrases to such an extent! There are no allusions in any of these family letters that need even mildly puzzle a stranger. They paint a fairly obvious picture – rather like the haversack letter twenty years before – 'I sent you a telegram'. But real letters are full of obscurities to a third person. The letter from Lloyds is hardly such as would be sent to a serving officer of Major's rank in wartime on an apparently static overdraft. It is not usual to expect the client himself to work out the complicated interest due on an overdraft. Bankers usually suggest a regular remittance from pay to reduce an overdraft, and to threaten proceedings for a sum of that size in wartime is most unusual.

If we are to be keenly critical I would quarrel with the Gieves bill; for it is perforated with a paid stamp. Now Gieves are most large in their credit terms to naval and marine officers, and I would hardly have expected Major Martin, with a severe letter from the head branch of his bank in his pocket, to be paying cash for such purchases. I should certainly not have done so.

Again the solicitor's letter is unusual in its wording to those used to receive solicitor's letters; for no solicitor would mention a legacy being made to 'your batman'. He would meticulously mention the name of the beneficiary. Moreover no Royal Marine officer in initiating such a correspondence would speak of his 'batman', for that is an army word, and the officers of the Royal Marines are waited upon, as all the world should know, by 'M.O.A.s' or Marine Officers' Attendants. (The banker's letter was not written by a banker; the solicitor's letter was not written by a solicitor.) These are perhaps small blemishes but such might lead to discovery, or at any rate to sufficient doubt to neutralise the whole plan. The reader may well ask also whether there was not grave risk of some enquiry being made in England by enemy agents. Why should not a German spy or a neutral agent be instructed to examine the hotel register of the Black Lion at Mold for the name of Martin, or telephone to the Naval and Military Club and ask for him, or even telephone as from casualties branch to the Royal Marine Office, only to discover that there was no such person in the Royal Corps.

Such perils I mentioned to the hush man, while expressing my admiration for the thoroughness with which this rather feckless personality had been built up.

The hush man said:

'It was agreed at the outset that such an operation as this could not have been risked, if the Germans had possessed a workable intelligence organisation in this country.'

So there was no serious threat from the secret organisations of Admiral Canaris, S.S. Senior Group Leader Kaltenbrunner or Joachim von Ribbentrop?

This then was the documentation that was at last approved, and then pocketed and packaged about the corpse. All the time, while the living acquired headed note-paper from writing desks and invested him with a letter-written character, the dead man lay in a morgue-freeze, waiting for his marching orders. Was it all proof against discovery?

TELEPHONE, WHITEHALL 9400.

WAR OFFICE,

WHITEHALL,

LONDON, S.W.I.

23rd April, 1943

<u>PERSONAL AND MOST SECRET.</u>

My dear Alex -

     I am taking advantage of sending you a personal letter by hand of one of Mountbatten's officers, to give you the inside history of our recent exchange of cables about Mediterranean operations and their attendant cover plans. You may have felt our decisions were somewhat arbitrary, but I can assure you in fact that the C.O.S. Committee gave the most careful consideration both to your recommendation and also to Jumbo's.

     We have had recent information that the Bosche have been reinforcing and strengthening their defences in Greece and Crete and C.I.G.S. felt that our forces for the assault were insufficient. It was agreed by the Chiefs of Staff that the 5th Division should be reinforced by one Brigade Group for the assault on the beach south of CAPE ARAXOS and that a similar reinforcement should be made for the 56th Division at KALAMATA. We are earmarking the necessary forces and shipping.

     Jumbo Wilson had proposed to select SICILY as cover target for "HUSKY"; but we have already chosen it as cover for operations "BRIMSTONE". The

/C.I.S.

General the Hon. Sir Harold R.L.G. Alexander,
    G.C.B.,C.S.I.,D.S.O.,M.C.,
      Headquarters,
        18th Army Group

C.O.S. Committee went into the whole question
exhaustively again and came to the conclusion
that in view of the preparations in Algeria, the
amphibious training which will be taking place on
the Tunisian coast and the heavy air bombardment
which will be put down to neutralise the Sicilian
airfields, we should stick to our plan of making it
cover for "BRIMSTONE" - indeed we stand a very good
chance of making him think we will go for Sicily -
it is an obvious objective and one about which he
must be nervous. On the other hand, they felt there
wasn't much hope of persuading the Bosche that the
extensive preparations in the Eastern Mediterranean
were also directed at SICILY. For this reason they
have told Wilson his cover plan should be something
nearer the spot, e.g. the Dodecanese. Since our
relations with Turkey are now so obviously closer
the Italians must be pretty apprehensive about these
islands.

I imagine you will agree with these arguments.
I know you will have your hands more than full at the
moment and you haven't much chance of discussing future
operations with Eisenhower. But if by any chance you
do want to support Wilson's proposal, I hope you will
let us know soon, because we can't delay much longer.

I am very sorry we weren't able to meet your
wishes about the new commander of the Guards Brigade.
Your own nominee was down with a bad attack of 'flu
and not likely to be really fit for another few weeks.
No doubt, however, you know Forster personally; he has
done extremely well in command of a brigade at home,
and is, I think, the best fellow available.

You must be about as fed up as we are with the
whole question of war medals and 'Purple Hearts'. We
all agree with you that we don't want to offend our
American friends, but there is a good deal more to it
than that. If our troops who happen to be serving in

/one

one particular theatre are to get extra decorations
merely because the Americans happen to be serving
there too, we will be faced with a good deal of
discontent among those troops fighting elsewhere
perhaps just as bitterly - or more so.   My own feeling
is that we should thank the Americans for their kind
offer but say firmly it would cause too many anomalies
and we are sorry we can't accept.   But it is on the
agenda for the next Military Members meeting and I
hope you will have a decision very soon.

Best of luck

Yours ever

Archie Hyp

V.C.I.G.S.
WAR OFFICE

COMBINED OPERATIONS HEADQUARTERS,
1A, RICHMOND TERRACE,
WHITEHALL S.W.1.

Telephone
WHitehall 9777

21st April,
1 9 4 3.

Dear Admiral of the Fleet,

    I promised V.C.I.G.S. that Major Martin would
arrange with you for the onward transmission of a
letter he has with him for General Alexander. It is
very urgent and very "hot" and as there are some
remarks in it that could not be seen by others in the
War Office, it could not go by signal. I feel sure
that you will see that it goes on safely and without
delay.

    I think you will find Martin the man you want.
He is quiet and shy at first, but he really knows his
stuff. He was more accurate than some of us about the
probable run of events at Dieppe and he has been well
in on the experiments with the latest barges and
equipment which took place up in Scotland.

    Let me have him back, please, as soon as the
assault is over. He might bring some sardines with him -
they are "on points" here!

yours sincerely

Louis Mountbatten

Admiral of the Fleet Sir A.B. Cunningham, G.C.B.,D.S.O.,
Commander in Chief Mediterranean,
Allied Force H.Q.,
Algiers.

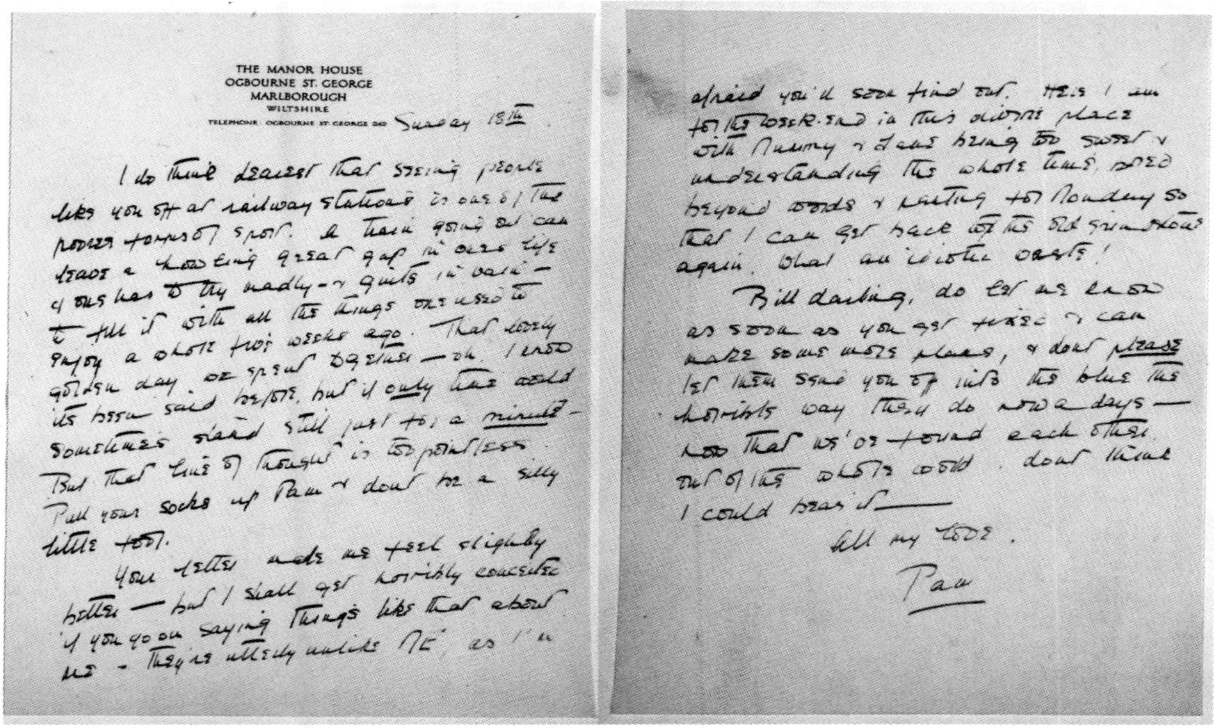
THE MANOR HOUSE
OGBOURNE ST. GEORGE
MARLBOROUGH
WILTSHIRE
TELEPHONE: OGBOURNE ST. GEORGE [illegible]

Sunday 18th

I do think dearest that seeing people like you off at railway stations is one of the rottenest forms of sport. A train going out can leave a howling great gap in one's life & one has to try madly – & quite in vain – to fill it with all the things one used to enjoy a whole four weeks ago. That lovely golden day we spent together – oh I know it's been said before, but if only time could sometimes stand still just for a minute – But that line of thought is too pointless. Pull your socks up Pam & don't be a silly little fool.

Your letter made me feel slightly better – but I shall get horribly conceited if you go on saying things like that about me – they're utterly unlike ME, as I'm afraid you'll soon find out. Here I am for the week-end in this divine place with Mummy & Dad being too sweet & understanding the whole time, bored beyond words & waiting for Monday so that I can get back to the old grindstone again. What an idiotic beast!

Bill darling, do let me know as soon as you get there & can make some more plans, & don't please let them send you off into the blue the horrible way they do nowadays — now that we've found each other out of the whole world. don't think I could bear it —

All my love.

Pam

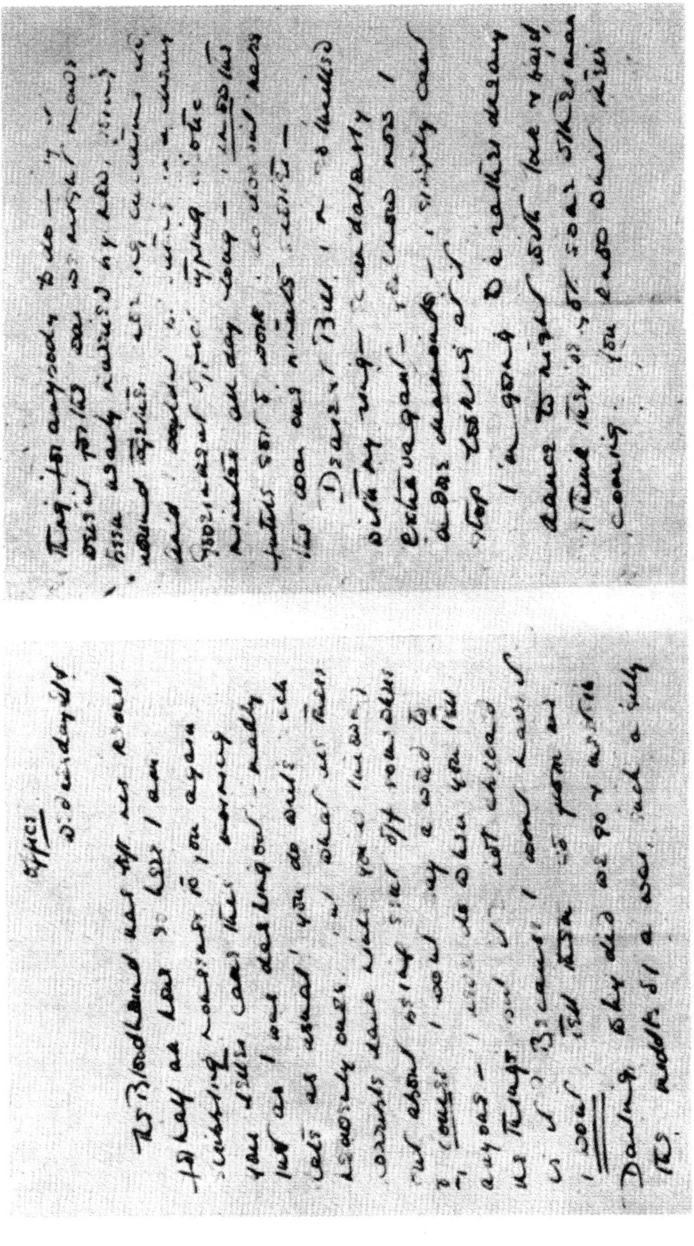

My dear William,

I cannot say that the hotel is any more comfortable as I remember it to have been in pre-war days. I am, however, staying here as the only alternative to imposing myself once more upon my aunt whose depleted staff I did not regard for the present leisure. I think I may be necessary over time. I have made the hotel almost unsuitable to a guest, at least as I myself propose to be in April or my age. If the 20-21st of April when no doubt we shall have an opportunity to meet. I enclose the copy of a letter which I have written to my solicitor Mackennis about your affairs. You will see that I have asked him to lunch with me at the Carlton Club (which I understand is still to be open)

at a quarter to one on Wednesday the 21st. I should be glad if you would make it possible to join us. We shall not however wait beyond one 20. Trust that if you are able to come, you will make a point of being punctual.

I asked John whom Priscilla had remembered to my own. She has grown into a sensible girl though I cannot say that her work for the Land Army is one much to improve her looks.

On that respect I am afraid that she will take after her father's side of the family.

Your affectionate
[signature]

BLACK LION HOTEL
MOLD.
N. WALES.
10 April

My dear Llewellin,

I have considered your recent letter concerning the settlement which I intend to make on the occasion of William's marriage. The provisions which you outline appear to me reasonably except in one particular. Since it is the case that the whole family will not be contributing to the settlement I do not think it proper that they should necessarily preserve after William's death as I am providing I should as in this case only over these children unless the settlement was so framed that the settlement and other children reported to be so arranged children the same reported to see any and should such

that and all remains or the children and may after their death the children who should benefit.

I intend to be in London on the two next days, the 20th + 21st April. I should be glad if you could make it convenient to take luncheon with me at the Carlton Grill at a quarter to one on Wednesday 21st. If you will bring the new draft with you we could have discussed and examine it afterwards. I have written to William in hope that he will be able to join us.

Yrs sincerely

(signed) R. Llewellin

T.M. Llewellin Esq
14 Kenna Rd
14 Lincoln's Place
London SW1

Lloyds Bank Limited.

TELEGRAPHIC ADDRESS.
"GUARDIANS, STOCK, LONDON."
TELEPHONE N?
MANSION HOUSE 1500.

POSTAL ADDRESS.
G.P.O. BOX 215,
71, LOMBARD STREET, E.C.3.

IN REPLYING PLEASE ADDRESS
THE JOINT GENERAL MANAGERS.

HEAD OFFICE,
LONDON, E.C.3.

14th April, 1943.

PRIVATE.

Major W. Martin, R.M.,
    Army and Navy Club,
      Pall Mall,
        LONDON, S.W.1.

Dear Sir,

        I am given to understand that in spite of
repeated application your overdraft amounting to
£79.19s.2d. still outstands.

        In the circumstances, I am now writing to
inform you that unless this amount, plus interest at
4% to date of payment, is received forthwith we shall
have no alternative but to take the necessary steps
to protect our interests.

        Yours faithfully,

        Joint General Manager.

PRIVATE.

LONDON E.C.
3 PM
14 APR
1943
E

Major W. Martin R.M.,
Army and Navy Club,
Pall Mall,
LONDON, S.W.1.

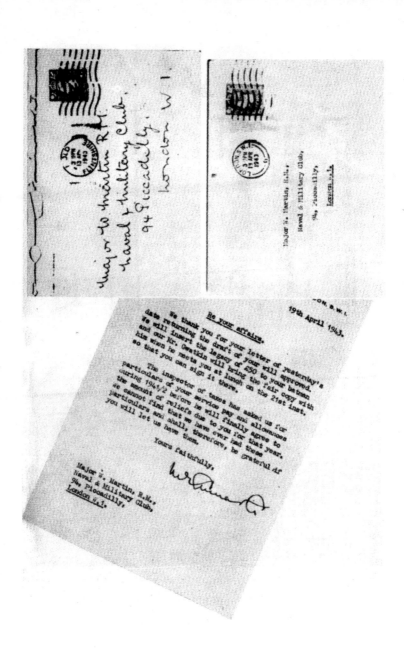

94, Piccadilly,
London W 1

Major W. Martin, R.M.,
Naval & Military Club,
94, Piccadilly,
London S.W.1

19th April 1943.

Re your affairs.

We thank you for your letter of yesterday's date returning the draft of your will approved. We will insert the legacy of £50 to your batman and our Mr. Gwatkin will bring the fair copy with him when he meets you at lunch on the 21st inst. so that you can sign it there.

The inspector of taxes has asked us for particulars of your service pay and allowances during 1941/2 before he will finally agree to the amount of reliefs due to you for that year. We cannot find that we have ever had these particulars and shall, therefore, be grateful if you will let us have them.

Yours faithfully,

Major W. Martin, R.M.,
Naval & Military Club,
94, Piccadilly,
London S.W.1.

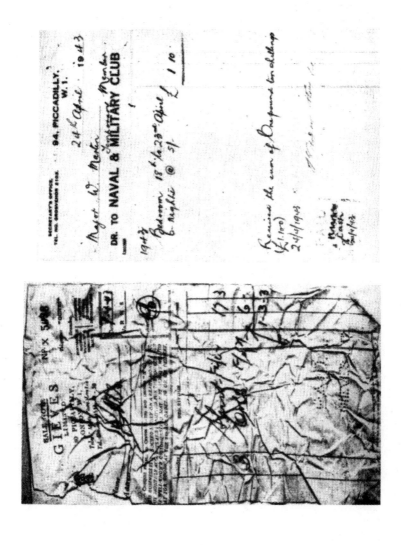

SECRETARY'S OFFICE.
TEL. NO. GROSVENOR 3106.

94, PICCADILLY,
W.1.

24th April 1943

Major W. Martin

DR. TO NAVAL & MILITARY CLUB

1943
Bedroom 18th to 23rd April
6 nights @ 5/-   £ 1 10 -

Received the sum of One pound ten shillings
(£1.10.0)
2/4/1943

Issued in lieu of N⁰ 09650 lost.

Surname MARTIN

Other Names WILLIAM

Rank (at time of issue) CAPTAIN, R.M.
                        (ACTING MAJOR)

Ship (at time of issue) H Q
              COMBINED OPERATIONS

Place of Birth   CARDIFF

Year of Birth 190

Issued by *C. Langene*

At

Date 2nd February 1943.

**NAVAL
IDENTITY CARD No. 148228**

Signature of Bearer

Visible distinguishing marks
        NIL.

[The photograph on the identity card is not of the man whose body was used for the operation]

PASS   No. 649.
COMBINED OPERATIONS HEADQUARERS

On presentation of this Pass the holder

Major W. Martin, R.M.

is authorized to enter on official duty
Combined Operations Headquarters.

                        Kenneth ...
                                Secretary.

Not valid after 31st MARCH, 1943.

This Pass is not transferable. If found, it should
be handed in at any Police Station, or sent to—

The Secretary,
    Combined Operations Headquarters,
        1A Richmond Terrace,
            Whitehall, S.W.1.

Signature of holder W. Martin

Further to the request which you recently made, on being introduced here, for a personal invitation card to be issued to you, this is now being prepared.

Should you, in the meantime, wish to attend any of the nightly parties held here, would you please present this letter at the reception desk. Any errors in the addressing of this letter should be notified to us without loss of time so as to avoid such mistakes being made on the invitation card.

Dancing commences at 11 p.m.   Cabaret at 1.30 a.m.

Telephones: Gerrard 6862
                 4623   CARD ISSUED No. *11120*

TELEPHONE Nº MAYFAIR 6261 (2 LINES)
TELEGRAMS EUCLASE WESDO LONDON.

113 New Bond Street
London. W. 1. 19th April 1943.

Major W. Martin, R.M.,
Naval & Military Club,
94 Piccadilly . W. 1.

To S. J. Phillips.

Silversmith.

Jewels. Antique Plate. Bijouterie.

15th April. 1943.	Single diamond ring small dia shoulders flat + (pre purchase tax)		52	10	-
	Engraving "P.L. from W.M. 14.4.43"			10	6
		£ 53	-	6

135

10

MAJOR MARTIN'S LAST VOYAGE

The backroom deliberations on Major William Martin in Whitehall are no concern of mine. But I am concerned that he should make a good impression on the world, since he had been enlisted in a fine corps that, alive or dead, has always served its country.

I do not know yet who Major Martin really was, and I have no proof when he really died. It has been said in Mr Ewen Montagu's account of his service that he died in the autumn of 1942. If so, that is a material point in our story.

Was he then dead even before Operation 'Torch' won for us the North African coast? He must have lain for months in the care of the Secret Service while the intelligence team was working out Operation 'Mincemeat', referring it to the Chiefs of Staff and for weeks also building up the personality and background of the dead man. So he was discussed and criticised at all levels.

At last the exhibits that we have seen were forged and approved, his uniform battle-dress was fitted to him, his brief-case fastened to the belt of his raincoat with a chain so arranged that he appeared to be clasping it in one hand. Then he was settled into the cool container and carbon dioxide was pumped in on the advice of Sir Bernard Spilsbury to keep decomposition from setting in. The British courier was ready for his last voyage.

What did he look like? I have been shown photographs of Major Martin taken just before he was put in the container, and these show a pinched and sunken face, a definitely tired look, reminiscent of some of the photographs of famines and massacres which find their way into the propaganda material of our times.

The container was put in an Admiralty vehicle in London and driven to Greenock, and then put on board the submarine *Seraph* commanded by Lieutenant N. L. A. Jewell, R.N. That is how the body left these shores.

The submarine Commander only had been briefed on the operation of all those sailing in *Seraph*, and at 6 p.m. on 19 April the *Seraph* left Holy Loch for the straits of Gibraltar and Algiers carrying the curious cylindrical container over six feet in length and the size of a large hot-water tank. Apart from Lieutenant Jewell nobody on board knew what this cylinder contained.

It had been discussed whether the operation should be carried out by an aircraft dropping the body, which would have had the advantage of speed, or whether a submarine should launch it. The latter method was chosen, because it allowed more precision in putting the body in the right spot. It avoided the risk of undue damage and post-death bruising to the body from a long drop into the sea. So the Royal Navy must do the job. Flag Officer Submarines, Admiral Sir Claud Barry was first consulted, and he had instructed the Commander of the *Seraph* to cooperate. The *Seraph* sailed submerged by day and surfaced at night, taking ten days from Western

Approaches to the Gulf of Cadiz, a distance that a liner in peacetime will cover comfortably in four days. The crew joked off watch about the mysterious container stowed in their ship.

The planners had selected the Huelva area for Major Martin's landfall, because it was far from Gibraltar. There was less danger of the courier's pouch being promptly offered to the British garrison of the Rock by friendly or gainful Spaniards. At Huelva, too, the set of the tides and the prevailing wind favoured the operation. It has also been said that there was an active German agent in Huelva, and that it was likely that he would manage to obtain the documents. All these reasons had been weighed, the dates fixed and certain precautions taken in Spain for the purpose of observing the safe arrival of Major Martin.

Lieutenant N. L. A. Jewell, now a Commander appointed to H.M.S. *Scorpion*, whom I contacted recently while in the Portsmouth command, was then twenty-nine years of age. He had already distinguished himself in Mediterranean operations, on 5 November 1942, in the embarking of General Giraud, who fled from Southern France to join the Free French. Jewell had also taken in the *Seraph* for the successful landing of General Mark Clark on the North African coast in October 1942, when General Clark carried out his daring political mission to meet French resistance agents before Operation 'Torch'.

The Admiralty publication *H.M. Submarines* tells the unusual exploits of Lieutenant Jewell and the *Seraph*. The third exploit, hitherto untold, was the strangest of all.

At 4.30 a.m. on 30 April, in darkness, on the turn of the ebb tide, Lieutenant Jewell had brought his submarine to a position off Huelva. He ordered the container to be opened on deck. On this April morning, his crew knew of this bulky passenger parcel only as an instrument container to be used in a secret research operation. The submarine commander briefed his officers on the meaning of the operation as the final act was about to begin. With all the crew below decks, it was an operation by hand of 'officers only'; for if ratings had been able to see what was done on deck, where might the secret deception plan have ended next time they reached port?

And what was going on that early morning of 30 April on the casing of H.M. Submarine *Seraph*? Dim figures working on the lid of the container, unbolting it with spanners. The watch-keeping officer had most to fear from enemy U-boats that at uncertain intervals crept through the straits of Gibraltar to attack Allied shipping in North African ports. Their routeing round the coast of Spain, out of reach of Allied aircraft, might bring them within striking range of the *Seraph* as she lay motionless there a mile and a half off the coast at Huelva. There was the danger too of a surprise by a Spanish warship or coastal vessel – in either case likely to endanger the whole operation.

Lieutenant Jewell may well have wondered, as a man with practical experience of the coast and the ways of sailors, how much luck and how much good management would play their part in this elaborate operation thereafter. The Spanish fishermen of Huelva, whose boats they later saw, would hardly be ardent supporters of the Axis cause. They would perhaps take the brief-case to the British Consul ashore for a tin of tobacco. They might pilfer the corpse and sink it with its precious papers. On the other hand the Spanish authorities ashore might behave with perfect propriety and return the papers unopened either to the British Vice-Consul or to the Governor of Gibraltar. Did anything make it certain that at this stage the operation would not miscarry entirely with dire consequences?

Had there been sufficient study of the Catalina accident near Cadiz in the previous November? Then the German agents in Cadiz had known of the accident and genuine most secret British orders had lain for hours unclaimed in the tunny-canning factory near Barrosa. What made Huelva any different from Cadiz?

It has been said that had the operation failed through the papers being lost altogether or returned unopened, another operation could have been mounted. What, another body with another build-up of its false identity and another set of documents? To judge by the time required to mount such an operation this was not an operation to be attempted again, once it had failed. Corpses could not be continually sent floating in with papers attached to them.

When the canister lid had been removed at that early hour on 30 April and the tapes securing Major Martin in his blanket had been released, Lieutenant Jewell had cause for concern. According to his patrol report active decomposition had set in. A green mould covered the lower half of the face of the unknown corpse. There was a strong putrefaction. Sir Bernard Spilsbury had been over confident in his claims for a container filled with carbon dioxide.

The canister carried by H.M.S. *Seraph*

Lieutenant Jewell inspected the Mae West, saw to it that the briefcase was secure on the chain and in the clutching fingers of the courier, and then the body was gently shoved off the submarine casing into the sea. Further off, they launched a rubber dinghy and one paddle, evidence upon which the Spanish naval authorities in Cadiz might try to reconstruct the accident.

Jewell's orders were to sink the container-coffin in deep water, and this he attempted to do. Air was trapped in it and it decided to float! There was no alternative but to sink it with small arms fire as it rolled alongside.

The *Seraph* sent a signal: 'Operation "Mincemeat" completed.' Then she made for Gibraltar, and Lieutenant Jewell sent back to the Admiralty the following patrol report.

MOST SECRET
From the Commanding Officer, H.M. Submarine *Seraph*.
Date: 30th April, 1943.

To Director of Naval Intelligence.
Copy to F.O.S.
(For Lt. Cdr. The Hon. E. E. S. Montagu, R.N.V.R.) Personal.

Operation 'Mincemeat'

1. *Weather*: The wind was variable altering between SW and SE, force 2. It was expected that the sea breeze would spring up in the morning, close inshore, as it had on the previous morning in similar conditions. Sea and swell – 2.0. – Sky overcast with very low clouds – visibility was patchy, up to 2 miles – Barometer 1016.

2. *Fishing boats*: A large number of small fishing boats were

working in the bay. The closest was left, about a mile off, and it is not thought that the submarine was observed by them.

3. *Operation*: The time of 0430 was chosen as being the nearest to low water Lisbon (0731), which would allow the submarine to be well clear by dawn. The canister was opened up and the body examined. The brief case was found to be securely attached. The face was heavily tanned and the whole of the lower half from the eyes down covered with mould. The skin had started to break away on the nose and cheek bones. The body was very high. The Mae West was blown up very hard and no further air was needed. The body was placed in the water at 0430 in a position 148° Portil Pillar 1.3 miles approximately eight cables from the beach and started to drift inshore. This was aided by the wash of the screws going full speed astern. The rubber dinghy was placed in the water blown up and upside down about half a mile further south of this position. The submarine then withdrew to seaward and the canister, filled with water, and containing the blanket, tapes and also the rubber dinghy's container was pushed over the side in position 36°37' 30 North 07°18' 00 West in 310 fathoms of water by sounding machine. The container would not at first submerge but after being riddled by fire from Vickers gun and also .455 revolver at very short range was seen to sink. Signal reporting operation complete was passed at 0717. A sample of the water close inshore is attached.

N. L. A. JEWELL
Lieutenant-in-Command.

Major Martin had now reached the most precarious stage of his venture. Hitherto he had been guarded and cosseted by his friends.

Nothing had been too good for him. No pains had been too great to make him seem a regular marine officer. But the Atlantic tide flowing inshore was now taking him within the reach of the enemy, and what might prove to be more dangerous still, the dispassionate eye of the neutral Spaniard. And the ordinary Spaniard was neutral, for all that is said to the contrary of certain politicians in Madrid and the paid agents and official liaison officers who worked with the Germans. What cared the Andalusians in remote Huelva for the heady philosophy of 'blood and soil' or the doctrines of the *Herrenvolk*? This neutral, easy-going, proud people with its strict sense for correct behaviour might prove the undoing of Operation 'Mincemeat'. For what was the real history of this body?

It had lain for months in refrigeration after dying a natural death. These were its movements.

Died autumn 1942.

Kept frozen until circa 15 April 1943.

Embarked in container 19 April 1943.

Half a day in sea 30 April 1943.

The Spaniards and the Germans would be expected to believe that this body had:

Died from shock or drowning 24 April 1943.

Floated in the sea for seven days.

For the earliest date of the 'accident' could only be 23 April; the telltale theatre ticket stubs in his pockets for *Strike a New Note* at the Prince of Wales Theatre on 22 April and gave him no chance of an alibi. He must have been in London on 22 April.

The movements of the man had been too rigidly laid down for him; so intent were the officers in London on making it appear that he had been the victim of an aircraft accident, that they had placed on the body this 'evidence' that he had been in London a few days previously. Not evidence in the absolute sense of the word, since anybody can buy tickets in advance and tear off the stubs, but proof anyway to all except a criminologist.

So loaded with circumstantial papers, complete with his accreditation, Major Martin floated on with the inshore breeze.

There were complicating medical factors.

Long preservation on ice leads to blue pinching, a tingeing of the skin, and intense contraction of the surface blood vessels. These symptoms the body showed.

What was the condition of the lungs? An expert could have pumped brine into stomach and lungs to fake drowning. This was not done. Death from shock might be presumed instead. Of the liquid left in the lungs by pneumonia – since it has been said that Spilsbury approved a pneumonia corpse, let me cite medical opinion – that liquid, *pleural effusion*, can hardly be mistaken for sea water.

Of rigor mortis there was no sign, though as the body had allegedly been in the water for a week, that would be taken to have passed off; but the symptoms that a corpse bears after a week in salt water, the bloated discoloured appearance, might not appear. It might not need a specialist of the calibre of Sir Bernard Spilsbury, or his German rival, Professor Mueller-Hess, to give an opinion that there was something strange about the body of Major Martin. A lay man might guess – the Vice-Consul or the Spanish naval authorities. What of the doctor who would perform the autopsy? He would certainly have seen other corpses that had been really drowned in the Gulf of Cadiz!

The intrepid Major floated on, carrying his gigantic bluff with him, towards the harbour bar and the mouth of the Rio Tinto.

The sun shone on the stone of the wharves and warehouses of Huelva. It was strong sunshine that reared the palm heads in the avenues and plazas.

For thirty years, as long as the British Vice-Consul, Mr Francis Haselden, could remember, there had but once been ice in Huelva, paper-thin on the puddles, and twice only snow. That thirtieth day of April, it was already hot as the hottest midsummer day in England.

The war had been an active time indeed for the British Vice-Consul; for although the shipping of ore had fallen from 2,000,000 tons yearly to only 1,500,000, there were so many additional precautions to be taken. Sea captains had to be warned to get out lights at night and keep watches in harbour and in the river against frogmen dropping downstream with limpet bombs.

Gibraltar had to be notified of every ore ship sailing. The ore ships must go to Gibraltar and join convoy there for England. They had to be de-loused for limpet bombs, if the captains had been long ashore at nights or careless in setting their harbour watch. All this the Vice-Consul had to consider and act upon.

He knew the Chief of Police well; he knew the naval and military commandants of Huelva. The naval commandant, a Commander of the Spanish Armada, was subordinate to the Admiral at Cadiz. The military commandant was responsible to the Captain-General at Seville. Thence all responsibilities ran to Madrid.

The Vice-Consul was perturbed at the activities of the Germans and Italians with their frogmen equipment and their pre-set time-bombs. He knew that the Germans, who could no longer trade from Huelva themselves, would seek to sabotage British seaborne trade – the sulphur, the ore, the pyrites that went to our war effort. He suspected the German agent in Cadiz of working with the staff of the Admiral, and with the German colony in Huelva.

The German Consul was a blind old man, but his two sons were active about the port. They met the German mining engineers, they knew the Spanish watchkeepers at the harbour bar. They knew when British shipping came and went.

The Spanish watchmen on the harbour bar had a telephone to the harbourmaster's office.

They reported the finding of a drowned body on 30 April, the body of a British officer.

It was known too to the Germans in Huelva that a package had been attached to the body.

Mr Haselden was telephoned and told of the find – another body, more work for the British Consul.

It was a hot afternoon, and the body was taken straight to the morgue of Huelva cemetery outside the port. There it lay on a trestle table, a sodden corpse.

Beside it lay a black brief-case; both the Vice-Consul and the staff officer to the naval commandant of Huelva eyed this brief-case.

The belongings of the body, his personal papers, his identity discs, the contents of his pockets were examined.

A port medical officer arrived at the cemetery for the autopsy, for which the Vice-Consul gave his permission.

How hot it was, and stifling in the small morgue building. The doctor set to work on his autopsy. The Vice-Consul went out for some fresh air.

'Asphyxia – death by drowning,' said the doctor, who was glad to be shot of the job.

'Yes, obviously drowning,' said the Vice-Consul.

He had seen many such drowned corpses in his consular days, and this looked no different to him from any other.

The body was placed in the coffin that the Vice-Consul had ordered. There lay the black brief-case.

'You will be taking this, no doubt,' said the Spanish officer.

'I think it should be deposited with the naval commandant for the night,' said the Vice-Consul. 'I will come and take it over officially in the morning.'

The Spanish Commander took the brief-case pensively, and pensively he returned to the office of the naval commandant. Once or twice before, in special circumstances, the British Vice-Consul had left British property in the care of the Spanish Navy at Huelva.

When the Vice-Consul called on the naval commandant next morning, the Spaniard informed him that the brief-case had been forwarded to the Admiral at Cadiz. What a surprise!

There was nothing more for Mr Haselden to do, but send off a telegram to Madrid reporting the incident.

He hired a priest to read the burial service, and the Spanish officers, with the courtesy that is proverbial in the Spanish, came to the bright sunlit cemetery outside Huelva on the hill at the end of the cactus lane.

There beneath the palm trees and the shrubs in a brick tenement, they buried Major William Martin, on 2 May 1943, and the Vice-Consul inscribed his death in the register as I found it ten years later.

As this was a British officer, he paid for the grave in perpetuity, and ordered a tombstone.

Meanwhile there was lively concern in Madrid and London about this incident. The British naval Attaché in Madrid received a signal from the Admiralty:

To: N. A. MADRID (Personal)
MOST SECRET IMMEDIATE
From: D.N.I. (Personal)

Your 678157. You should request immediate return of papers which are most secret.

Documents when obtained to be sent unopened by quickest means to me.

If documents not surrendered to you institute enquiries particularly as to whether they came ashore with body.

394732.

This was followed shortly by a second signal:

To: N. A. MADRID (Personal)
IMPORTANT MOST SECRET
From: D.N.I. (Personal)

My 394732.
Report as soon as possible whether despatch case washed up with body.

Case normal official pattern bearing Royal cypher. If discovered return at once.

If not take care to see that it is recovered if it is washed up subsequently.

895920.

The Ambassador in Madrid, Sir Samuel Hoare, was instructed to press for immediate return of the documents which he did with the characteristic vigour that he showed in all his diplomatic dealings.

There was at first no response. The dilatory and haphazard processes of Spanish officialdom covered the whereabouts of the documents. The black brief-case had gone from Huelva to Cadiz, to Seville, to Madrid.

At what stage the Germans first came into the enjoyment of Major Martin's papers will never be quite certain. The story of Lenz is frank enough.

I asked the old man to think again after sending him copies of the documents that he had been chasing ten years previously. The sight of them refreshed his memory.

'Ach, it comes back a little now,' he murmured. He recalled details from the dossier on the case that he had destroyed at the end of the war. 'The first to report on this drowned courier was not our Huelva man,' he said.

It was our intelligence officer in Cadiz. He has since died, but I can vouch for it that he was not expert enough to have pierced deception of that kind. He simply reported the facts as he saw them. As I have already said, I sent on my photostats to Berlin, by special courier, without adding an opinion on them, because I could not quite overcome my professional wariness. Yet I had nothing to disprove the documents.

The documents were in any case valuable to me. They showed me firstly that a landing in Southern Europe from Africa was really being planned. Whether it was to be Sardinia first, or Sicily or the Peloponnese was of lesser importance. It gave me an indication on which to check your convoy movements.

I recall now that there was a query from Berlin – I think that Berlin was suspicious about the incident – and that we asked the Cadiz agent for a description of the circumstances in which the body was found. His second report gave further details about the body and its personal effects, and I sent it on to Berlin. After that there were no more enquiries!

So the personal papers of Major Martin had been scanned, and his letters had doubtless been read, but not scrutinised with the eye of a connoisseur. Nobody had gone from Cadiz to Huelva to enquire of the pathologist or the Spanish naval staff officer in what condition the corpse had been found. That was the vital omission.

The doctor did not know what papers the dead man had carried, or he might have wondered that a man who had enjoyed a musical show in London on 22 April should come out of the Atlantic so badly decomposed on the 30th.

The Spanish naval officer who knew the reported date of the accident – 24 April – may not have asked for the opinion of the doctor on the body. It seems that he did not even inform Cadiz that the British Consul had been remiss in claiming the documents.

So one official omission followed another. It is only in fiction that every move is noticed.

One word, one hesitation might have started a train of thought; Lenz might have communicated his suspicions to Baumann, and discovered that his Special Operations officer was a medical jurist and an expert pathologist.

Baumann might have found someone to invite the Spanish naval officer to lunch, and, in the course of easy conversation, the questions might have been asked by a languid hostess.

'Commander, what happened to this courier's papers?'

'We sent them to Madrid.'

'Did not the British Vice-Consul demand them back?'

'In fact, Madam, it was the British Vice-Consul who allowed that these papers should be lodged with El Commandatore.'

'Permit me, Commander, to help you to a little more sherry. And what struck you about the condition of this body?'

'Madam, the air is close today. Let us withdraw a little on to the patio.'

So it would have gone in a novel, but in reality life is full of missed opportunities. Agents soon lose the enthusiasm for ranging that enlivens the dust jackets of fiction. They become sedate and blunted. They work from paper and theory.

But some clues were there, if the Germans had been alert enough, or if the Spaniards had in fact been helping them as much as some people liked to believe.

There was scope for a counter-operation to 'Mincemeat', a body snatching by moonlight, and Major Martin would have gone on another long journey; this time to Berlin – a conundrum from Spilsbury for Mueller-Hess to solve.

I personally think Mueller-Hess would have solved it, but if we judge from results the first phase of the deception was successful.

Nobody noticed a flaw in the text of the banker's letter, or the law-yer's letter to Major Martin. They may have looked realistic in their brine-stained condition. Nobody had apparently read Wavell on Allenby, or the Official History of the Palestine Campaign or Sir George Aston on the refinements of the Secret Service!

Rigor mortis was setting in with the German Military Intel-ligence Service. It was relying too much on the desk report and the telephone call; it dealt too much in official hand-outs from the liaison officers of host powers; it spent a lot of its time seeming to conspire against Hitler, thwarting his worst excesses, or try-ing to hold its position and prestige against the active rivalry of Kaltenbrunner's Security Service.

I met Mr Francis Haselden living in retirement in Surrey after the war. He was able to confirm to me some details of my account of the happenings in Huelva. He had heard with interest that I had just been in Huelva.

He had also read, so he told me, a novel that indeed resem-bled closely what had happened during his period as Vice-Consul in Huelva. It had been sent to him as a present, but he could not remember who had written it, or the title of the book.

'Was it *Operation Heartbreak*?'

'I believe so.'

'Was it written by Duff Cooper?'

'Yes that would be it. Now when I read that book, I thought – this is curious – a courier's body with papers was washed up in Huelva during my time. It's all very like it.'

'And what did you think when you saw the body?'

'I thought that he looked like any other drowned corpse I had seen.'

Thus spoke the reserved Mr Haselden. I found myself puzzling as to his role in this operation. Was it his seeming negligence that prevented the whole operation from failing? But neglecting his consular duties was by no means the mark of Haselden. Not a single British ship of all those that left Huelva during the war had been sunk by sabotage. He knew his business. He knew Huelva like the palm of his hand. Did I detect a shrewd twinkle in the eye of the Vice-Consul? Let me just say here that I do not think that anything in this operation was left to chance!

So Major Martin was accepted into the society of the dead. His credentials were not put to the test of criminology. His letters in photostat were flown on to Berlin.

But would these dispatches be lost in the mass of other conflicting intelligence reports? Would some sceptical person in 'Foreign Armies West' Branch of the German General Staff discover discrepancies and gradually get at the truth? Let us see what Hitler was told and how he reacted!

II

HITLER HEARS
ABOUT MAJOR MARTIN

Adolf Hitler became more morose as the year 1943 wore on. At a conference of 14 March with the Commander-in-Chief of the German Navy, Admiral Doenitz, he could see that Generals Eisenhower and Alexander were closing on Tunisia and the Afrika Korps. Rommel had counterattacked three days before against General LeClerc's Free French at Ksar Ghilane, but without much effect.

'Tunisia strategically is of prime importance,' said Hitler. Everything seemed to be of prime importance when he was about to lose it.

There listened to the vegetarian strategist in the 'Wolf's Lair' at Rastenburg a respectful audience of Field-Marshal Keitel, his Chief of High Command, Field-Marshal Kesselring, his Commander-in-Chief Southern Front, Air General Jeschonnek, Lieutenant General Jodi of the High Command's Operations Staff, Admiral Doenitz, Commander-in-Chief of the Navy, three Rear-Admirals and a naval captain.

'Tunisia is strategically of prime importance,' he said.

> Conquest of Tunisia means a saving of 4–5 million tons and more to the enemy, so that the submarines have to work 4–5 months to effect equalization. Retention of Tunisia is a question of supplies. The 80,000 tons per month cited as necessary by the Italian Supreme Command are entirely inadequate; rather 150,000 to 200,000 tons monthly are needed. We estimate for each division about 1 train – 500 tons daily. For the 8 divisions in Tunisia, inclusive of the Italians, this makes a total of 4,000 tons daily.

The upshot was that Admiral Doenitz was sent to Mussolini to ask for an all-out Italian convoy effort, without which Tunisia would be lost. 'Restraint and disapproval' was what Doenitz noted on the faces of the Italian admirals in Rome, though when the talk turned to Sardinia the Duce said that he would commit the entire Italian fleet to prevent an Allied landing there.

Throughout March and April the naval victories of the Allies in the Mediterranean piled up. The cruiser *Trieste* was sunk in a Sardinian port, the cruiser *Gorizia* was damaged, the Allies closed on Tunis. Rommel flew back to Germany to report to the Führer and was kept there. General von Arnim surrendered the German forces on the Cape Bon peninsula. Doenitz in despondency spoke at the Führer's conferences of the imperative need to build more U-boats. He asked for an invasion of Spain and an attack on Gibraltar.

On the day before von Arnim surrendered on the Cape Bon peninsula, 12 May 1943, Hitler sent Doenitz to Rome for a second series of conferences with the Italians. This time it was the defence of the northern shores of the Mediterranean that mattered. Africa was lost.

As he flew south the Admiral's mind was absorbed with the future strategic problem. It had not yet been answered by the German

Military Intelligence Service. When he met his three flag officers in Italy, Rear-Admiral Ruge, Rear-Admiral Meendsen-Bohlken and Rear-Admiral Loewisch, he raised the puzzling question:

'Which is more important – Sardinia or Sicily? Which will the Allies attack?'

The four admirals pondered on that. They lunched together and discussed their own problems of overlapping in their respective Mediterranean naval commands – a problem which seems constantly to beset the navies of this world. Admiral Doenitz drove after lunch to the Italian admiralty. Admiral Riccardi, the Italian Commander-in-Chief, received Doenitz with courtesy and explained to him what Italian intelligence showed.

'The enemy is preparing for further operations from the Algerian harbours,' said Riccardi; 'at the same time he is systematically destroying the Italian harbours. Since the fall of Tunisia an attack on the Italian islands is expected any day.'

Rear-Admiral Sansonetti interpreted the views of the Italian Admiralty staff.

Until the enemy can make use of the harbours of Bizerta and Tunis, there is no reason to expect an invasion of Sicily. Of course the enemy knows of the minefields between Sicily and North Africa. As it would take perhaps a month to sweep these minefields, an invasion of Sardinia is to be considered more likely at this moment. The Italian Admiralty believes that Sardinia will be the first to be invaded. An invasion of Sicily may be expected some time after June 22nd.

It was arranged that Admiral Doenitz should call on Mussolini on 13 May to discuss defence of the Mediterranean islands and shores. What did the Duce think?

As Marshal of the Imperium and Supreme Commander, he had sent General Ambrosio, Chief of Staff of the Armed Forces, to inspect the defences of Sardinia as soon as Tunisia fell, and General Ambrosio had written him a penetrating report, of which he can still be proud.'[17] It is dated 8 May 1943, after the calculated rumours of an Allied attack on Sardinia had begun to be 'fed' into Axis intelligence channels.

'During my visit to Sardinia,' wrote Ambrosio to Mussolini,

I was once more obliged to ask myself whether the theory that the enemy would try to seize the island was a tenable one or not.

A landing in Sardinia would not be an easy matter; the stretches of coast which lend themselves to such a landing are few and narrow; the hinterland is difficult; we could bring aeronaval opposition heavily to bear on the convoys and decimate them; supplies would suffer the same fate; and our land defences are not to be underestimated.

The enemy might reckon with a high percentage of losses, but he would at least want to be sure of success. Not only would this assurance be lacking, and thus the risks great, but the severe losses which he must in any case suffer should at least be compensated by the importance of the objective.

Now Sardinia is not an object of capital importance in the strategic picture of the Mediterranean.

Unless the Anglo-Americans intend to invade Italy, in which case, acting consecutively, i.e., without a break, they might even conquer Sardinia to make it a springboard for invasion, I do not see an adequate proportion between the aim of the operation and its difficulty.

17   *Mussolini Memoirs.*

I do not believe in an invasion of the mainland because it would be a long affair and would not decide the final result of the war; Italy, even if reduced to the Po Valley, would not give in; our adversaries must know this by now.

All things considered, I believe that the chances of an attack on Sardinia are remote, and in any case I think them much slighter than the chances of an attempt to invade Sicily whose strategic position in the Mediterranean presents a far greater obstacle to our enemies. The conquest of Sicily need not presuppose a further operation against the mainland, but could be an end in itself, because it would give the enemy safety of movement and would lessen the engagements of his naval forces and the losses of his mercantile marine; that is to say, it is in itself an objective of real and preeminent importance, worth pursuing with all energy and at any cost.

In General Ambrosio, Major Martin had an enemy worthy of his mettle. Mussolini was inclined not to fear for Sardinia. Of the divisions that Hitler offered him, he told Doenitz how he proposed to place the tank battalions – with an emphasis on Sicily.

'The Duce,' wrote Doenitz,

is well, optimistic, composed, very frank, sincere and amicable.

The Duce states that he is confident about the future. The only result of British air raids on Italy will be that the people will learn to hate the British, which has not always been the case. This helps in carrying on the war. If there is one Italian who hates the British, it is he himself. He is happy that his people are now learning the meaning of the word hate as well.

He has answered the Führer's offer of five divisions, by stating he wants only three of them. This refusal came as a surprise to the

Commander-in-Chief, Navy. The Duce explains that he had asked that these three divisions should include six armoured battalions with 300 tanks, *two of which are detailed for Sardinia, three for Sicily and one for southern Italy.* He believes that Sicily is in the greatest danger and supports his contention by referring to the British press which had repeatedly stated that free route through the Mediterranean would mean a gain of 2,000,000 tons of cargo space for the Allies.

Doenitz drove on to the Headquarters of Field-Marshal Kesselring, Commander-in-Chief of German troops in Italy. Doenitz noted:

> On his tour of inspection in Sicily the Commanding General, South, has noticed that Italian defence preparations were very incomplete. We had therefore impressed this fact on the Italian Commander-in-Chief, General Roatta. A similar tour of inspection of Sardinia is planned during the next few days.
>
> The Commanding General, South, agrees with the Duce that an attack on Sicily is more probable than an attack on Sardinia.

So we see that Doenitz gathered from his Italian visit that Sicily was the likelier target. At no time indeed did Mussolini openly alter this view. As for Doenitz, he did not commit himself yet. No doubt the Führer would have the answer. And the Führer did!

On 14 May, Doenitz flew home and reported to Hitler at his Rastenburg Headquarters in East Prussia. The Italians were obviously weakening, said Doenitz, and he had little faith in their promises. Hitler too began to have doubts about Fascist loyalty to the Axis.

Then Hitler gave Admiral Doenitz an intriguing morsel of news.

A British Admiralty footnote to the Allied edition of the *Führer Conferences* states that the military problem of where the Allies would next strike was still unsolved. While Doenitz was in Italy, however, an Allied order had been discovered and shown to Hitler, pointing to Sardinia and the Peloponnesus as the next Allied objectives. At the conference between Hitler and Doenitz, Hitler showed that he accepted this information as true and laid his plans accordingly.

Now the rapid tour of Doenitz in Italy had only taken two days, and the information had not reached him in Berlin before he started. So plainly it had taken just a fortnight from 30 April, when the body of Major Martin reached Huelva, for his documents to be copied and brought to the notice of the Führer.

With what excited interest Hitler told the Commander-in-Chief of the German Navy of the accident to the British courier and the stroke of fortune that had played these papers into his hands, the British editor of the *Führer Conferences* does not reveal. And perhaps Doenitz himself was too security-minded to enlarge on such a secret source of intelligence in his dictated notes. But the account of their conversation, fragmentary though it may be, gives us clear proof that the ruse had worked on Hitler at any rate.

Report to the Führer at Headquarters, Wolfsschanze.

14th May 1943 at 1730.

The Commander-in-Chief, Navy reports the progress and outcome of his conference with the Duce.

He adds, that while the Duce did not disapprove of concentrating all efforts on the transport of supplies, no action was taken as the result of the Commander-in-Chief's report. The Führer believes that the Duce partly rejected the offer of several German divisions under the influence of the Italian High Command, in order to keep a free hand.

The Führer does not agree with the Duce that the most likely invasion point is Sicily. Furthermore, he believes that the discovered Anglo-Saxon order confirms the assumption that the planned attacks will be directed mainly against Sardinia and the Peloponnesus.

The Commander-in-Chief, Navy then reports on his conference with the Supermarina and mentions the places on Sardinia and Sicily where the Italians believe landing attempts will be made.

Hitler and Doenitz pondered how lasting the loyalty of the Duce might be. They discussed the submarine war and that operation which Hitler had often desired but shied at doing by force – the march through Spain to attack Gibraltar. Then they decided to allocate supplies of 200,000 tons monthly to Sicily and 80,000 tons monthly to Sardinia, which, whatever its danger, was less populated and had fewer places to defend.

So ended the conference in which Hitler reviewed his strategy in the light of Major Martin's intelligence.

The German naval war diary and the diary of the Army High Command are captured documents and as such not available for scrutiny, according to a British cabinet ruling, until the official war historians have finished with them. When they do become known, they will show that both Army and Naval Staff at once accepted the interpretation that Sardinia was the next target. In the deployment of German forces to meet the Allied threat a German armoured division was moved from France to the Peloponnesus, commanding those beaches named in the Nye 'letter'.

Eleven days later the story of the drowned courier's papers was subjected to a keener scrutiny, when Dr Goebbels discussed with Admiral Canaris, Chief of German Military Intelligence, indications of the next Allied move in the war.

I had a long discussion with Admiral Canaris about the data available for forecasting English intentions. Canaris has gained possession of a letter written by the English General Staff to General Alexander. This letter is extremely informative and reveals English plans almost to the dotting of an 'i'. I don't know whether the letter is merely camouflage – Canaris denies this energetically – or whether it actually corresponds to the facts. In any case the general outline of English plans for this summer revealed here seems on the whole to tally. According to it, the English and Americans are planning several sham attacks during the coming months – one in the West, one on Sicily, and one on the Dodecanese islands. These attacks are to immobilize our troops stationed there, thus enabling English forces to undertake other and more serious operations. These operations are to involve Sardinia and the Peloponnesus. On the whole this line of reasoning seems to be right. Hence, if the letter to General Alexander is the real thing, we shall have to prepare to repel a number of attacks which are partly serious and partly sham.

The passionate Doktor was a better judge here than the experienced old intelligence officer, most of whose time was devoted to preventing Nazi encroachments in the intelligence field, but if Canaris had been unable to resist the bait, Goebbels on another occasion had swallowed it too.

On 13 May 1943 Goebbels noted in his diary that Colonel Frank Knox, U.S. Secretary to the Navy, had publicly declared that Sicily would be occupied next.

'We pay no attention to these unfounded rumours and attempts at deception,' he wrote. They annoyed Mussolini also, these politicians trumpeting to the Allied press. Perhaps in the overall deception plan for Operation 'Husky', in which Major Martin played a subordinate if important role, it had been agreed between Britain and America to give speculation a free rein. The more publicly Sicily was proclaimed to be the next target, it might be argued the more Hitler and Mussolini would tend to believe the forged indications that Sicily was only a 'cover target'.

Mussolini had been turning over these possibilities. In a 'note on the strategic situation in the middle of June', presented to his War Council at the Villa Torlonia on 14 June 1943, he wrote:

> Enemy tactics – in order to assist the war of nerves – consist in giving the press and radio free rein in any hypothesis concerning the Second Front, even the most absurd and fantastic.
>
> But under cover of this noisy though harmless babble the enemy's political and strategic conduct of the war is obeying the laws of geography and the rule of the maximum result with minimum effort. Thus the attack on the Italian islands in the central Mediterranean was fatally obvious – because it was logical. Thus, too, we may anticipate a further action against the other Italian islands in the Mediterranean, Sicily, Sardinia and Rhodes. All this cannot yet be called an invasion of Europe, but it would be the necessary prelude to it. And this may perhaps fill the bill for 1943.[18]

So the Duce was still not allowing himself to be drawn. It is interesting that just three days later, on 17 June, Mr Churchill became rather perturbed at the vocal Allied press forecasts on the next step in the Mediterranean.

'I am anxious about deception plans for Sicily,' he wrote in a minute to General Ismay for the Chiefs of Staff Committee.

18 *Mussolini Memoirs.*

The newspapers all seem to be pointing to Sicily ... this objective would seem to be proclaimed and common property.

Safety lies in multiplication and confusion of objectives. A helpful note seems to have been struck this morning in some papers in saying that we have sufficient forces to attack several objectives at once ... Surely Greece requires some prominence?[19]

This was three weeks before the assault on Sicily began. Let us then look at as much of the deception plan as has been revealed, and see who was fooled and how.

This strategy of attack and feint is best described in the simplest words by Mr Churchill in *The Hinge of Fate* and *Closing the Ring*, and it is interesting to note that his appreciation of the relative importance of Sicily and Sardinia agrees with that of General Ambrosio.

'The Second immediate objective (after Tunis),' he had written on 25 November 1942, 'is obviously either Sardinia or Sicily ... Note that the preparations to attack Sardinia may take as long as those to attack Sicily, and that Sicily is by far the greater prize.'[20]

He described Allied cover plans as keeping the enemy in doubt until the last moment where the stroke would fall. Allied naval movements and military preparations in Egypt suggested an expedition to Greece. 'Since the fall of Tunis they (the Axis powers) had sent more planes to the Mediterranean but the additional squadrons had gone, not to Sicily, but to the Eastern Mediterranean, north-west Italy and Sardinia.'[21]

These reactions certainly fitted the pattern of our deception.

19 *The Second World War*, Vol. V, p. 567.
20 Ibid., Vol. IV, p. 587.
21 Ibid., Vol. V, p. 31.

General Eisenhower shows in his *Crusade in Europe* that to support the deception, the naval task force, Force H, manoeuvred and bombarded off the coast of Greece.

From Cairo and Switzerland, after the attack on Sicily began, the rumours of an impending attack on Greece were spread persistently. The name of Mr Churchill was bandied about and the suggestion that he personally was hankering after an advance through the Balkans. We find Hitler in the third week of July switching Rommel over to Greece to organise the defences there, Mr Desmond Young tells us, because of 'a rumour that Mr. Churchill was about to stage an invasion of Europe through the Balkans'.[22]

And in *The Rommel Papers* there is the following diary entry by Rommel on 23 July:

'Long discussion with the Führer. I am to report in detail and direct to him on conditions in Greece. Forces there, besides Eleventh Italian Army, include only one German armoured division (1st Panzer Division) and three infantry divisions.'

Two days later he records arriving in Salonika in 'terrific heat'.

We find these same rumours mentioned in Hitler's military conference of 25 July, at the height of the crisis in Italy, while Mussolini was being hustled out of public life in a military ambulance.[23]

We even find this 'plant' still accepted as an historical fact in the post-war memoirs of German generals,[24] deprived of their own documents and unversed in the military annals of the Allies.

Obviously the overall deception plan could not be served by one operation alone, fascinating and successful as Operation

22 *Rommel*, p. 187.
23 *Hitler Directs His War*, p. 52.
24 General Siegfried Westphal, Chief of Staff to Kesselring, mentions 'Churchill's plan for a Second Front in South-East Europe' (*The German Army in the West*, p. 200). General Hans Speidel, later Rommel's Chief of Staff, mentions it also as a product of the first Cairo Conference (*We Defended Normandy*, p. 31).

'Mincemeat' was. One 'plant' after another had to keep up the delusion, disperse the enemy strength and keep it dispersed.

I can state on good authority that a Balkans front, once it was clear that Turkey would not fight, was never seriously considered by Mr Churchill.

So the German armoured division that was moved in May 1943 from France to the Peloponnese, and the German naval forces sent from Italy to Greek ports to face a ghost invasion were kept there by an infinity of tricks, swallowed by the penetrated and defeatist German intelligence services of Admiral Canaris.

How powerful an impression the ominous corpse of Huelva had made on Hitler himself may be gathered from the record of the Führer's conference of 11 August 1943, with Admiral Doenitz and Field-Marshal Rommel, a full month after the invasion of Sicily.

After Rommel and Doenitz had opposed Jodl's idea for pulling out of Sicily and defending the mainland, Hitler declared his belief 'that the enemy will not attack the Italian mainland if Italy remains loyal, but possibly Sardinia. However his intuition tells him that Italy is planning treason.'

The dazzled Doenitz wrote down an afterthought:

Note by the Commander-in-Chief, Navy: The enormous strength which the Führer radiates, his unwavering confidence, and his far-sighted appraisal of the Italian situation have made it very clear in these days that we are all very insignificant in comparison with the Führer, and that our knowledge and the picture we get from our limited vantage are fragmentary. Anyone who believes that he can do better than the Führer is silly.

Six weeks later Doenitz was still warning his Führer that the next Allied attack would be directed against South-East Europe.

And what had in fact been the fortunes of the day in Sicily? Bad weather and a heavy swell on 9 July had put the garrison off its guard. 'The very efficient cover plan and the deceptive routeing of convoys had played their part,' wrote Admiral of the Fleet Sir Andrew Cunningham. Air power and the assault of two Allied armies carried the island in thirty-eight days. Of 405,000 Axis troops, 167,000 had been killed or captured for the loss of 31,000 Allied troops killed, wounded and missing.

And long after the Allies gathering their strength leapt across the Straits of Messina on to the mainland on 3 September, thoughts of the mythical Balkans plan still haunted the Germans. After even the Salerno landings, Admiral Doenitz noted confidently on 25 September in his record of a Führer conference:

'The next strategic moves of the enemy are evidently directed against the Balkans.'

12

CONCLUSIONS

Did the Germans ever recognise the fakes? Were the letter from General Nye to General Alexander and the letter from Admiral Mountbatten to Admiral Cunningham finally classified as clever forgeries? In the absence of any evidence, I think not. When the war was over, and tongues were loosened, it was another matter.

The story began to creep about. It appeared in German memoirs years afterwards, a hearsay story.

The letters were so carefully phrased that no amount of study could prove them false. Lenz, ten years afterwards, still said they had been valuable to him as an indication of Allied intentions. That was the finest tribute of all.

You will have noticed some weaknesses in the planning – possibly too much prose in the pockets of the corpse. The condition of the body too might have contradicted the official version of his death.

Let us allow for the difficulty of legally obtaining disposal of a body in such a manner. It matters not whether in peace or war, you cannot help yourself to a body in England at short notice.

I am nevertheless inclined to think that there was some official complacency towards this body. I mean that he was treated rather like a filed application, to be brought up regularly once a month for review.

With much the same complacency hundreds of British officials consider it natural to keep food in cold storage for months, until gradually a nation loses all memory of the taste of fresh food.

Eventually, it may be imagined, there was a certain personal affection towards the man, and the planners would have been loth to accept any substitute.

How would the Germans have done such an operation? I remark first that Hitler was so unpredictable that elaborate strategic deception was not possible. Nobody could have been quite sure that it would not be true the next day.

But Heinrich Himmler would have provided a magnificent corpse. No month-old cadavers for him! Out of the wealth of material in the concentration camps, a true Nordic type would have been selected.

He would have been made to put on his own uniform. Gas chambers? Nothing so crude!

The public memory cannot be so short that the cold water immersion experiments are not remembered. In these, Himmler used 'criminal types' – by his own standards – to test the resistance of the human body to extreme cold and to improve on methods of resuscitation. He discovered eventually that human warmth, provided by gipsy women and other 'racial undesirables', was the most efficacious reviver of the circulation.

What would then have been more natural than to select a candidate for the cold water immersion experiments and finally to immerse the unconscious form in real earnest. This would have overcome the chief problem of getting a suitable corpse with water in the lungs.

Par excellence this was a German operation, and one which it is hard to imagine the lackadaisical British putting into practice. That was one of the beauties of it – who would ever have thought that the British would do that?

Well, they know now and by some it is considered a pity that they should. Such an opinion was voiced in the House of Commons on 18 March 1953.

The member for Gosport asked the Ministry of Defence what motive had led to the publication of this story with its secret aspects. Mr Birch replied that nothing harmful to security had been printed, and with that the subject appeared to be closed.

It was interesting to learn that the ministerial decision to allow publication was taken in principle before my search for Major Martin started.

Doubtless, however, this ruse must follow the haversack ruse into oblivion. Not less spectacular in its conception, with a classic sureness of touch, it was perhaps not quite so decisive in its effect.

For I am not one of those who think that Major Martin won the war for us, though he may well have saved thousands of lives by helping to spread the German defence. I have yet to learn that he displaced any Italian divisions; for Mussolini understood better than Hitler where the threat to the Italian heartland lay. It was a matter of geographical fact. But then the placing of Italian divisions mattered less. A creature of corpses and omens himself, the Austrian Macbeth was the more gullible of the two.

I have heard with fascination from one of the men concerned with the inception of Operation 'Mincemeat', that such a sceptical frame of mind was induced in the Germans by this hoax as may partly explain Ribbentrop's and Kaltenbrunner's deep mistrust of the 'Cicero' haul – the photostats of British 'Most Secret' papers extracted from the residence of the British Ambassador in Ankara late in 1943 and early in 1944 by his valet, a German spy.

If that can be proved, then Major Martin was a security agent as well as a deception man, and is owed a debt of gratitude by MI5.

Surely too next time there is an accident to a British courier and his papers are lost, nobody will treat them very seriously. So even out of the glare of publicity that has attended the revelation of what he did, some good may come in the end.

I think that some claims that have been made on his behalf would astonish Major Martin. His answer would be simply that he did nothing that any other fellow could not have done in his place. That is – having once got over the astonishment of finding himself in such unaccustomed surroundings.

You will ask me too whether the Russians would have been satisfied with the intelligence that Major Martin presented. I am no expert on Russian psychology, but I believe them to be by nature mistrustful and not easily given to thinking that fortune has put an amazing gift of information in their way.

The German intelligence service was a bureaucratic outfit. It had no strong roots abroad. The Soviet intelligence service can call upon the cells of the Communist party everywhere. I can imagine that it would not have been long before they had put a few systematic checks on the Major and his landfall, through dock workers, through minor officials. At any rate they would not have accepted him as *bona fide* as quickly as the Germans did. That was just one of those curious traits in the German character of always accepting the Englishman as a perfect gentleman, in which they are occasionally disappointed.

You will be thinking that the reading of this story will tend to be painful to the Spanish regime. That is why I have been particularly careful to go into what happened in Huelva; for if it is decided by H.M. Ministers to sanction publication of the truth about a secret incident of the war, then let us in fairness to all have the whole truth.

For that reason I would emphasise that there was at first no mad scramble by the Spaniards in Huelva to relieve the Major of his important-looking brief-case. I have also asked the British Vice-Consul to confirm whether he in fact did leave the brief-case overnight with the port commandant.

His reply, with a dry smile, was, 'No comment.'

And if this brief-case was opened, we do not know when or by whom. Let it be remarked that Major Martin was not a King's Messenger. He enjoyed no diplomatic immunity.

Finally, do you imagine that those British officials who planned Operation 'Mincemeat' would themselves have been squeamish under similar conditions of photographing the documents found on a foreign corpse in unexplained circumstances on these shores? Enough said!

'I am authorised to tell you,' said a Spanish official, 'that General Franco, as soon as he heard of this incident gave strict orders that the brief-case was to be returned to the British Embassy in Madrid unopened.'

So indeed would any British Prime Minister have said, and perhaps also it might already have been too late.

As to the documents or photostats of the documents being shown to the Germans, well, that is hard to stomach. Offset against it, perhaps, the silence of the man who carried the brief-case from Huelva cemetery to the port commandant's office.

Let me also say that at no point in my quest was there any attempt on the part of Spanish officials to hinder or deflect me. The whole business was regarded in the light of a sporting venture.

And if we used this plum of deception tricks so early on, what had we left for the Normandy operations, you will ask, when so much more was at stake? Was there anything left in the bag? Should not Major Martin have been swum in before Operation 'Overlord'?

Well, to judge by results, there was still plenty in the bag. Not the haversack ruse or the body, but others! A game fish will find live bait irresistible. And live bait it has always been and always will be in the war of intelligence and deception. As long as new generations are unwilling to learn by anything but their own mistakes, there will always be successful deception.

It fell to me recently to be translating into English the memoirs of Rommel's last Chief of Staff, Lieutenant-General Dr Hans Speidel,[25] and long the General and I puzzled over essential discrepancies between his version of the British order of battle and that which was to be found in the accounts of Field-Marshal Montgomery and General Eisenhower.[26]

Earnestly we searched for the explanation to the large reserve of divisions with which the General credited the Allies. Certain German movements in the field and particularly the unwillingness of Hitler and Rundstedt to reinforce Normandy from the Pas de Calais armies pointed once more to a calculated plan of deception on a grand scale.

It was Eisenhower himself who put General Speidel wise to his errors in a friendly meeting years afterwards in France.

'Why,' said Ike, 'you have given me ten divisions that I never possessed!'

All the time ghost divisions had moved or concentrated, according to the faulty reports reaching the German intelligence service, and they seemed to offer a constant threat of another massed

25 *We Defended Normandy*, by General Hans Speidel.
26 *From Normandy to the Baltic, Crusade in Europe.*

landing in the Pas de Calais. It never came. Thus in 'Overlord' deception once more tied down many German divisions.

As to live bait, well I wouldn't put it past the hush men to send a clumsy agent to reconnoitre the wrong area on the strong likelihood that he would be caught there. You will say that this is hardly fair, and my reply to that is that the looking-glass dimension through which we have stepped to see how enemies deceive each other in war has very little room for the philosophy of the cricket field. And once again I say that there seem to be as many variations as you can imagine, and that even the repetition of a ruse leaves the victim wondering whether the enemy can really be such a fool as to repeat himself.

All the same, I do feel with tolerable certainty – as certain as anybody can feel in this uncertain dimension – that the trick which Major Martin played in Huelva will not be repeated. His personal dossiers and the vexed correspondence that has gone on about him at Cabinet level has made him, though gratitude and affection still exist towards him, a man whose performance will not be emulated by others.

We have got thus far, and now you will be asking me a very natural question – who was he?

That is a natural question. Even in this well-ordered country it is a little surprising to know that things like that can happen, justifiable and authorised though they may be.

I am not bound to accept a published explanation that he was a hospital casualty in military service, whose next of kin gave permission for the operation. In that case I think a more decorous appellation than Operation 'Mincemeat' could have been found for it; nor do I accept that this was the codename that lay next on the list, and so was used.

So I am inclined to think that the mysterious man who had the honour to save so many lives was no more than one of the many obscure dead who have no place in society, the unknown persons who so frequently crop up in the records of coroners. That is simply my theory on such slender evidence that there is. Of course, it may be that I shall discover who he was from Sir Bernard Spilsbury's files, or something about him, and not be permitted to tell you. If that happens, you must recollect that the silent intelligence services have really been most accommodating in this extraordinary case, and that if they use the faint blue pencil that so seldom marks an author's script in this country, we can hardly blame them for it.

13
POST MORTEM

'WELL you have been away quite a time, but you found the body,' said the vicar. 'I was telling you before you left for Spain of my own sermon about the difficulty of hiding a body, one of the wartime sermons I preached to the Royal Marines.'

I said, 'The body was in this case an advantage to the operation and an encumbrance afterwards.'

'In that particular sermon to the Royal Marines,' said the vicar,

I enlarged on the difficulties of hiding a body. Clever men have often failed to do so and years afterwards the bodies have turned up to confront them with a crime.

Think on the other hand of the complete disappearance of a body overnight that is never found again, though the whole priesthood of a nation was intent on discovering where it might be, with the full assistance of the civil power!

'Ah, there you have a much more important story than mine,' I ventured. 'Mine simply leads to the successful end of one campaign in one year in a problematical war.'

Yet looking back my search was an enlivening experience. The quest in Spain with its unforgettable sunsets, the quiet moments among sunlit tombs, the vigour of life in the bodega of Seville, the grandeur of Gibraltar, a frown or a smile to all who pass into the Mediterranean! And then a long conversation in the restful siesta of the day with a footsore priest in the wide Andalusian plain. Here and there on the horizon lay his parish, and straightly he questioned me whether there were bicycles in Gibraltar, and what they cost, and whether a bicycle might be brought into Spain without much difficulty. Something of his importunity moved me, the simple desire to get round a little faster in the slow measured life of that land for the comfort and succour of those who lived in it.

You have heard about the 'Who-done-it' in this case. You are naturally waiting for the 'Who-was-it' – was Major Martin soldier, sailor, rich man, poor man, beggarman? That is not really material to our story and I am told that there is no clue to his name, even in the voluminous card index that Sir Bernard Spilsbury kept. So I must leave the courier unknown.

Thus the man who in England would probably have filled an obscure grave went into his little niche in history. The hazards of the operation sometimes take our breath away but by its success it must ultimately be judged.

THE END

POSTSCRIPT

The answer to Colvin's question as to which of 'tinker, tailor, soldier, sailor, rich man, poor man' Major Martin really was, is certainly poor man, maybe even beggarman. The identity of the body was revealed in 1998, when the Ministry of Defence released the files relating to Operation Mincemeat. The body had been that of Glyndwr Michael, a 34-year-old Welsh man who had been living rough in London and had died after eating bread scraps which had been smeared with rat poison. As a result of the revelation, a sentence was added to the Huelva grave. It read:

Glyndwr Michael; Served as Major William Martin, RM.

APPENDIX

Here are a number of documents from the National Archives on Operation Mincemeat which was first proposed by the Double Cross Committee in February 1943.

OPERATION MINCEMEAT

This Operation is proposed in view of the fact that the enemy will almost certainly get information of the preparation of any assault mounted in North Africa and will try to find out its target.

1. Object.

(i) To pass to the enemy operation orders of an operation in the Mediterranean in such circumstances that they will regard them as the orders for the next operation to be carried out by the Allies.

(ii) To do this sufficiently early to affect enemy dispositions, and so that they attribute any actual preparations they will see to that operation and do not try to form an unguided appreciation which may be accurate.

2. Method of Deception.

(i) It is considered probable that, as a result of previous experiences, the Germans will be looking with care for our cover-plan as well as for our real plan. They should, therefore, be given two sets of operation orders, one purporting to be the real plan (which should have an approved 'cover' target) and the other purporting to be the cover plan (which should have another approved 'cover' target).

(ii) Operation Plan.
This should be drawn up so as to appear to be a draft of operation orders which are being sent to North Africa for comment and suggestions. The following points must be included:–

    (a) It should give a date about a month too early, so that it falls in with the visible preparations and, if submarines are concentrated, the enemy will not know for how long it has been postponed.

    (b) It should refer to the correct number of assembly points in North Africa, stating that they are in that country but referring to them as A, B, C, etc. This will cover agents' and recce reports without giving anything away.

    (c) It should either include forces from outside the Mediterranean (if it is decided to convey the impression that our forces will be stronger than exist in that area) but state that they are coming from the U.S. (not the U.K.) or omit reference to them (if it is desired to minimise our forces).

(d) It should either mention numbers of forces at the North African assembly points or not, according to whether a definite policy of either minimising or increasing troops to be used can be decided on or not. Although a preliminary draft, it would be much more likely to carry conviction if it could mention troops to be used, identifying units known by the enemy to be in North Africa.

(e) It should mention, particularising as far as possible, transports, special ships and escorts.

(f) If the real target is to be, say, Sicily, the target in this document should be, say, Sardinia.

(g) It should be given a code name.

(iii) Cover Plan

This should be drawn up on exactly the same basis as the 'operation plan' above, except that:–

(a) No units need be identified but numbers should either be increased or decreased throughout.

(b) A date a week, earlier or later than in the 'operation plan' should be given.

(c) A different but credible target should be given, say the Balearics and Marseilles, and give Sicily as an alternative for consideration (if the real objective and the 'operation order' objective are as in 2 (ii) (f) above).

(d) If Sicily is the real target and omitted from both the 'operation plan' and the 'cover plan' the Germans will almost certainly suspect as, not only is Sicily a very possible target, but the Germans are believed already to anticipate it as a possible target.

(e) It should be given a different code name.

Proposed Method of Passing to the Enemy.

A dead body, dressed in Officer's uniform, and carrying these and other papers, should be dropped from an aircraft, together with some portions of wreckage from a suitable aircraft, in a position whence it will probably wash ashore on Spanish territory. The impression to be conveyed being that a courier carrying important 'hand of officer' documents was en route for Algiers in an aircraft which crashed.

Prospects of Success.

(i) A suitable body has been obtained and is now available and can be used at any time within the next three months or so.

(ii) Expert opinion has been taken and it is not thought that the enemy would be able to discover that the body had died in some other way. This is made the more probable as the Spaniards will not be likely to hand the body over to the enemy (but to a British Consul) and do not approve of post mortems.

(iii) From experience it is considered that the Spaniards will probably allow the Germans to have photographs or copies of the documents. This will be the more probable if the Balearics are mentioned in the 'cover' plan and not in the 'operation' plan.

(iv) From experience it is considered that the Germans will believe these documents. This will be the more probable if we 'plug' the 'operation' target through credible channels and the 'cover' target through blown channels.

5. Difficulties.

(i) The body must be dropped within 24 hours of its being removed from its present place in London. The flight, once laid on, must not be cancelled or postponed.

(ii) The body will have to receive burial in Spain and enquiries as to identity, etc. will be received by the appropriate department of the Service in whose uniform it is dressed.

TWENTY COMMITTEE.

4. 2. 43

Lieutenant-Commander Ewen Montagu and Flight-Lieutenant Charles Cholmondley, who were the naval and air force representatives on the Double Cross Committee, put together a plan and, on 4 April 1943, Colonel Johnny Bevan, the head of the London Controlling Section which oversaw deception surrounding military operations, put the plans forward to the armed forces Chiefs of Staff.

MOST SECRET

Operation Mincemeat

Object

It is desired to place in the hands of the German Intelligence Service some really convincing information which will mislead them as to the objective of HUSKY.

Considerations

2. It is considered that one way in which this can be effected would be to plant on the enemy a high level document which should disclose:–

   (i) what purports to be the real objective.
   (ii) what purports to be the cover or deception objective,

3. It is probable that any document, purporting to be a British official document, which is washed ashore in the Huelva area of Spain will be handed over to the Germans, or at least photographed for them.

Plan

4. It is proposed to cause a dead body, dressed in British Officer's uniform, to be washed ashore in the Huelva area together with a bag (containing inter alia the document mentioned in para. 2 above) and other articles as if they had gradually been washed ashore after an aircraft crash while en route to AFHQ from England.

5. All arrangements have been made with the appropriate British authorities in Spain and the body has been prepared together with nil necessary documents and other 'properties' to lend verisimilitude. The operation will be carried out by H.M.S. SER-APH while en route for Gibraltar after leaving this country on 18th or 19th April. The probable date of the operation will be 28th April.

6. The crucial letter from Vice-Chief of the Imperial General Staff to General Alexander, giving the facts mentioned in para. 2 above, has been approved by Colonel Dudley Clarke who is in charge of the deception for HUSKY. The letter is considered to be one which will be accepted as authentic by the Germans for the following reasons:–

    (a) It is passing between persons who are not only 'in the know' but also on a high enough level to exclude the possibility of mistake.

    (b) The tenor and tone of the letter are such that the Germans are likely to accept it as an 'off the record' negotiation between two officers who are personal friends and working in harmony.

    (c) The purported real objective is not blatantly mentioned although very clearly indicated.

(d) The Germans will on this occasion be looking for a cover or deception objective and this is given to them.

(e) The purported cover or deception objectives include SICILY which they are already appreciating as one of the most probable of our real objectives, and will also explain our later preparations which may point more clearly to that island.

Recommendations

7. It is requested that approval should be given for the carrying out of this operation.

4TH APRIL, 1943.

The Chiefs of Staff agreed the plans and Bevan was summoned to brief the wartime Prime Minister Winston Churchill. He was shocked by the way in which he was received.

Most Secret.

MINCEMEAT.

I was instructed by Lt Gen Ismay to see the Prime Minister at 10 am on 14 April and explain Operation Mincemeat to him. To my surprise I was ushered into his bedroom (in his annexe) where I found him in bed smoking a cigar. He was surrounded with papers and black and red Cabinet boxes.

After explaining the scheme, in which he took much interest, I pointed out that there was of course a chance that the plan might miscarry and that we would be found out. Furthermore that the body might have got washed up or that if it did, the Spaniards might hand it over to the local British authority without having taken the crucial papers. "In that case" the P.M. said "we shall have to get the body back and give it another swim".

He agreed the plan but directed that permission for its execution must be obtained from Gen Eisenhower. This was duly obtained.

John H Bevan
Controlling Officer.

When the German intelligence reports relating to Operation Mincemeat were examined at the end of the war, they confirmed that the plan had worked perfectly, as explained here by Johnny Bevan.

OPERATION MINCEMEAT

As you will probably remember we had confirmation from C's Most Secret Sources and from subsequent actions of the Germans that they had swallowed the deception in MINCEMEAT.

Now further and more detailed comment on MINCEMEAT has come to light in the files of the German High Command. I attach a translation of a bundle of three documents, prepared for Admiral Dönitz, which were in the file on Mediterranean operations from 1.1.43 to 14.5.43 and they reveal in an interesting way the manner in which the Germans reacted to various points in the letter; examples are the stress on Tobruk as against Alexandria and the effectiveness of the rather weak joke about Sardinia which had been purposely included in the letter from Admiral Mountbatten to Admiral of the Fleet Sir A. B. Cunningham, K.C.B., D.S.O. It referred to the Major Martin who was carrying the letter and read: 'Let me have him back please, as soon as the assault is over. He might bring some sardines with him – they are "on points" here.' It is therefore clear that this letter was also read and had its deceptive effect, apart from its usefulness as 'build-up'.

I also enclose a copy of a report from the *Abwehr* [German Intelligence] on how the documents were discovered. It reveals, for the first time, that the minutiae among the personal documents on Major Martin's person all were examined and played their intended part. For instance the bill (actually theatre ticket stubs) dated 27th April, fixed, as was intended, his presence in London until a date too late for his to have reached Huelva by any other means than by aircraft.

It also reveals the degree of Spanish complicity: we know from other sources that this exchange of information with the Germans in fact took place on a high level in Madrid. The skill of the Spanish work in extracting the documents was not as great as the Germans thought: our postal censorship experts, who were especially consulted, deduced that at least one of the letters had probably been extracted from the envelope although none of the seals had been tampered with.

It may also be of some interest, although one cannot say it is definitely connected, that the next document on the file was an order from Hitler that a complete regiment, with its ancillaries and supplies for two months should go to Corsica. We, of course, already knew that a Panzer Division had been sent from France to the communications centre dominating the two specified beaches in the Peloponnese.

The German feeling that there might be an actual cover operation during the assault may account for the concentration of troops, defences, etc., at the western end of Sicily.

The first of the three German intelligence reports attached to Bevan's note was sent to Admiral Karl Dönitz, the head of the German Navy, on 14 May 1943, two weeks after the body washed ashore.

SUBJECT: CAPTURED ENEMY DOCUMENT ON MEDITERRANEAN OPERATIONS.

Attached herewith are:–

(a) Translation of the captured letter from the Imperial General Staff to General Alexander.
(b) Appreciation thereof by the [German] General Staff.

The contents of further captured documents are unimportant, exhaustive elimination revealed the following:–

1. The genuineness of the captured documents is above suspicion. The suggestion that they have intentionally fallen into our hands – of which the probability is slight – and the question whether the enemy is aware of the capture of the documents by us or only of their loss at sea is being followed up. It is possible that the enemy has no knowledge of the capture of the documents. Against that it is certain that he knows that they did not reach their destination.

2. Whether the enemy will now alter his intended operations or will set an earlier date for their commencement must be taken into consideration, but seems unlikely.

3. Probable date of the Operation.
   The matter is being treated as urgent; yet there is still time on the 23rd April to inform General Alexander by air courier

of General Wilson's proposal to use Sicily as cover-target for the assault in the Eastern Mediterranean, wherein he is requested to reply immediately in the event of his supporting Wilson's opinion 'as we cannot postpone the matter much longer'. In this case the Imperial General Staff considers altering the planning both in the Eastern and Western Mediterranean, for which there is still time.

4. Sequence of the Operations.

It is presumed that both operations will take place simultaneously, since Sicily is unsuitable as a cover-target simultaneously for both.

The Tobruk area comes into consideration as a starting-point for the operations in the Eastern Mediterranean. Alexandria is not considered, as in this case Sicily would have been absurd as a cover-target.

It is not clear whether the deception worked by the cover-target concerns only the period up to the beginning of the operations or whether in fact a cover-operation would be used as well as the actual assault.

It is not clear from the attached whether only the 5th and 16th Divisions will be landed in the Eastern Mediterranean (at Araxos and Kalamata). However only those two Divisions are to be reinforced for their assault. It is always possible that all assault troops and targets are included with them.

It should be emphasised that it is obvious from this document that big preparations are in course in the Eastern Mediterranean as well. This is important, because considerably less intelligence about preparations has reached us from this area than from Algeria, owing to their geographical situation.

The second report was a signal sent to Admiral Dönitz from German naval intelligence.

Further to, my 2144/43 dated 9.5.43 following appreciation has been made on receipt of original material:–

1. A landing in the Eastern and Western Mediterranean on a fairly large scale is anticipated.
   (a) Target of the operation in Eastern Mediterranean under General Wilson is the coast near Kalamata and the stretch of coast south of Cape Araxos (both on the West coast of the Peloponnese). The reinforced 56th Infantry Division is detailed for the landing at Kalamata and the reinforced 5th Infantry Division at Capo Araxos. It is not known whether both divisions will land in force or in part only. In the first instance, a lapse of at least 2–3 weeks would be required as the 56th Division on 9.5.43. was engaged at Enfidaville with two brigades and must first be rested and embarked. This solution, which embraces a certain delay before the landing can take place, appears to be the more probable from the way in which the letter is written. However, if the landing is to be effected by only certain units of both divisions, it could be made at any time, as one brigade of the 56th Division and 1–2 brigades of the 5th Division are probably already available in the actual starting-area (Egypt–Libya). Code-name for the landing on the Peloponnese is 'HUSKY'. The Anglo-American General Staff has proposed a simultaneous cover-operation against the Dodecanese to General Wilson. Wilson's decision thereon was not yet taken on 23.4.43.

(b) Target for the operation under General Alexander in the Western Mediterranean is not mentioned. A joking reference in the letter points to Sardinia. Codename for this operation is 'BRIMSTONE'. The proposed cover-target for operation 'BRIMSTONE' is Sicily.

2. Maintenance of complete secrecy over this discovery and utmost limitation of circulation of this information is essential.

The final report was the Abwehr explanation of how the documents came into their hands and the confirmation of the complicity of the Spanish police.

SUBJECT: BRITISH OFFICIAL MAIL WASHED ASHORE NEAR HUELVA.

The following points were cleared up in a conversation on 10.5.43. with the official concerned, a Spanish staff officer with whom we have been in contact for many years:–

1. Clutched in the hand of the corpse was an ordinary briefcase which contained the following documents:–

   (a) A piece of ordinary white paper containing letters addressed to General Alexander and Admiral Cunningham. This white paper 'bore no writing on it'.

   Each of the three letters was in a separate envelope with the usual form of address and directed personally to the addressee, sealed apparently with the sender's private seal (signet ring).

   The seals were in perfect condition.

   The letters themselves, which I have had in my hands in their re-sealed envelopes, are in good condition. For reproduction purposes the Spaniards had dried them with artificial heat and then placed them in salt water for twenty-four hours, without greatly altering their condition.

   (b) Also in the brief-case were the proofs of the pamphlet on the operations of the Combined Operations Command mentioned by Mountbatten in his letter of 22nd April, as well as the photographs mentioned therein.

The proofs were in perfect condition, but the photographs were quite ruined.

2. The messenger also carried a note-case in the breast-pocket of his coat with personal papers, including his military papers with photographs (according to these he was the Major Martin referred to in Mountbatten's letter of 22nd April) a letter to Major Martin from his fiancée and one from his father, and a London night-club bill dated 27th April. Major Martin therefore left London on the morning of 28th April, the same day that the aircraft came to grief near Huelva.

3. The British Consul was present at the discovery and is fully informed about it. The expected suggestions by the British Consul that the documents should be handed over to him were set aside under the pretext that all articles found on the body, including all papers, must be laid before the local Spanish magistrate.

   After being reproduced, all documents were returned to their original condition by the Spanish General Staff; and definitely give the impression – as I was able to see for myself – that they had not been opened. They will be returned to the English today through the Spanish Foreign Office.

   Further enquiries are being made by the Spanish General Staff concerning the whereabouts of the pilot of the aircraft who was presumably injured in the crash, and an interrogation of the latter about any other passengers.

BIBLIOGRAPHY

Baedeker's Guide to Spain. Allen & Unwin.

Operation Heartbreak, Alfred Duff Cooper. Rupert Hart-Davis.

The Second World War, Vols. II, III, IV & V, Winston S. Churchill. Cassell.

Rommel, Desmond Young. Collins.

Ambassador on Special Mission, Sir Samuel Hoare. Collins.

The Rommel Papers, edited by Captain B. H. Liddell Hart. Collins.

The Goebbels Diaries, edited by Louis P. Lochner. Hamish Hamilton.

Mussolini's Memoirs, edited by Cecil Sprigge. Weidenfeld & Nicolson.

Revolt Against Hitler, Dr Fabian von Schlabrendorff. Eyre & Spottiswoode.

The German Army in the West, General Siegfried Westphal. Cassell.

We Defended Normandy, General Hans Speidel. Herbert Jenkins.

Chronology of the Second World War. Royal Institute of Foreign Affairs.

Führer Conferences on Naval Affairs. The Admiralty.

Hitler and His Admirals, Anthony Martienssen. Secker & Warburg.

Sir Bernard Spilsbury, His Life and Cases, Douglas Browne and E. V. Tullett. Harrap & Co.

Official History of the First World War. H.M. Stationery Office.
Allenby – A Study in Greatness, Lord Wavell. Harrap & Co.
Secret Service, Sir George Aston. Faber & Faber.
The Secret Corps, Captain F. Tuohy. John Murray.
Courage, Cyril M. Armitage. Frederick Muller Ltd.

INDEX

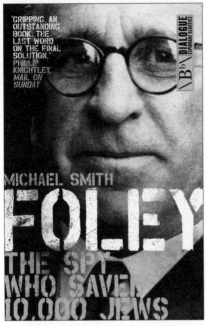

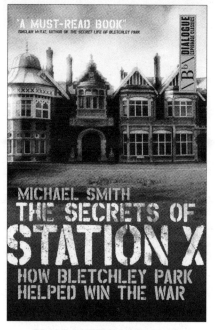

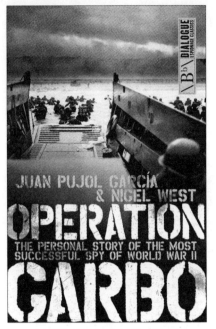